JESUS' ATTITUDE

TO

WEALTH AND POVERTY

JESUS' ATTITUDE

TO

WEALTH AND POVERTY

A REVOLUTIONARY NEWLOOK OF ITS IMPLICATIONS FOR THE
NIGERIAN CHRISTIANS

The Ven. Dr. Honest .U. Gad-Nwosu

iii

iv

DEDICATION

I dedicate this book to God Almighty, all the poverty stricken people of Nigeria and to my father - late Gad .N. Nwosu.

TABLE OF CONTENTS

ABBREVIATION

CBN	-	Central Bank of Nigeria.
IMF	-	International Monetary Fund.
NDLEA	-	National Drug Law Enforcement Agency.
NAA	-	Nigerian Airport Authority.
NEPA	-	National Electric Power Authority (Now NEPA PLC).
NIPOST	-	Nigerian Information and Postal Services.
NNPC	-	Nigerian National Petroleum Corporation.
NPA	-	Nigeria Ports Authority.
OPEC	-	Organization of Petroleum Economic Countries.
UNICEF	-	United Nations International Children Educational Fund.
US	-	United States.
VAT	-	Value Added Tax.
WHO	-	World Health Organization.

Jesus' Attitude to Wealth and Poverty

X

FOREWORD

I am delighted to write the foreword to this thought provoking book written by one of the Clergy men of the church of Nigeria (Anglican Communion) Serving under me in Enugu Diocese – The Ven. Dr. Honest Uche Gad-Nwosu. I have looked through the content and title and deemed it necessary to lend my fatherly support.

In this age of so many quests for materialism and less concern for the less privilege and the poor; this book has come to true love and compassion. The good news that is brought and preached by Jesus' is "The gospel to the poor; ---- to heal the brokenhearted, to proclaim liberty to the captives, and recovery of sight to the blind, to set at liberty those who are oppressed ..." (Luke 4:18). He was so committed to it that He said, "The blind see and the lame walk; the lepers are cleansed and the deaf hear; the dead are raised up and the poor have the gospel preached to them". (Matthew 11:5). But one wonders today, if the poor are hearing the gospel preached to them or rather being discriminated against.

Having gone through some biblical references to the poor and in line with the words of this book, I am fully convinced that the Bible has a special place and bias for the poor, which today's Christians have been neglecting. Jesus by words and actions shows that the poor have a special place in the plan of God. This was captured in the entire scriptures. Jesus looked with special compassion upon the poor.

In our nation today, there is much class distinction. Poverty is on the increase daily and no doubt a lot of people are living in abject poverty. If the government is not responsive to the needs of the poor and the neglected, should the church feel unconcern? The church, I mean Christian, in love should identify with and respond to the need of the poor. The church should not by any means neglect the poor.

This does not mean that Christians should not seek to prosper. It is biblical also to prosper. "Beloved, I pray that you may prosper in all things and be in health, just as your soul prospers". (3 John 2). There is no gain saying the fact, that Christian faithfulness generally brings material blessings. Christians should prosper; but as they prosper materially they should in the same vein, make conscious effort to reach out to the poor with the gospel, now that the resources are available to them. The "have" among Christians should help the "have-nots". Preachers and Christian leaders today by example and words should teach this biblical responsibility to Christians and help them act on it. This is not just for the poor themselves but also for the good of the wealthy. The Church needs the wealthy as well as the poor no one should be discriminated against. (James 2:2-4).

Reading this book, will provoke love and interest in Christians of our time to show much concern to the poor. It will also encourage Christians to seek to prosper in the right way, for poverty is not a virtue to be desired or prayed for.

As you read and apply the principles in this book as enunciate by this servant of God, I pray that you find yourself into the plan of God for you; as in, Jeremiah 29:11 "for I know the plans I have for you" declares the LORD, "plans to prosper you and not to harm you, plans to give you hope and a future" (NIV).

I recommend this book highly to all Christians who are conscious of the call of God upon their lives to spread the gospel of the kingdom. I also commend the painstaking work of the author of this book Honest Uche Gad-Nwosu whose ministry and Christian commitment I have followed closely for over twenty five years now. He has been a consistent follower of Christ and minister of the gospel. May you really be blessed.

The Most Rev. Dr. Emmanuel Olisa Chukwuma (OON)
Bishop of Enugu Diocese and Archbishop of Ecclesiastical Province of Enugu,
Church of Nigeria (Anglican Communion).

PREFACE

This is a six-chapter book which discusses Jesus' attitude to wealth and poverty, the implication for Nigerian Christians.

Wealth and Poverty have been issues of importance right from creation. The problem of Wealth and Poverty has been mostly on distribution. Right from the Old Testament, God laid a standard on how wealth should be distributed. This could be seen in the Jubilee Principle in Leviticus 25. God really has concern for the poor.

The incarnation of Jesus Christ is symbolic of God's concern for the poor. This is proclaimed by Jesus in his message in (Luke 4:18, cf. Isaiah 61). Jesus in his teaching made use of parables to express his attitude to Wealth and Poverty. Jesus showed a sort of bias for the poor, although he did not condemn or reject the rich. Poverty never originated from God. It is the result of the fall of man, man's selfishness and ultra-individualism. Jesus never idealized poverty rather he came to liberate the poor. This is what the Gospel is all about, that is, to establish a society in fellowship-<u>Koinonia.</u> Jesus became poor that humanity might, through his poverty, be made rich.

The Nigerian nation is blessed with abundant natural resources and fertile land, for everyone to live in comfortably. However, hunger is still written on the faces of many people. Something ought to be done to change things. The Christians in Nigeria should not live in or preach affluence while the majority of the population suffer in abject poverty.

The flamboyant preachers of today ought to consider their contributions to the eradication of poverty in Nigeria. A place is supposed to be given to the poor in the Church. Their voices ought to be heard in the affairs of the Church. The struggle for the liberation of the poor ought to start from the Church.

It is a heresy to teach that wealth is always a sign of righteousness and blessing. The righteous also do suffer. Wealth could as well come to one as a result of sinful acts but true wealth is that which is got through one's obedience to the rules of God. God wills justice for every man. There is a suggestion in this book for contentment and simplicity of life as an ideal way and the secret of inward peace. Wealth could be helpful as well as dangerous. Jesus advised on the need to avoid covetousness which is greed and avarice.

ACKNOWLEDGEMENT

I am highly appreciative of the painstaking and intellectual input to this book by my New Testament lecturer in the University of Ibadan, Rev. Professor S.O. Abogunrin. As my teacher, he contributed a lot to what I am now made of academically, other lecturer of mine, I must acknowledge their input are The Most Rev. S.L. Laisebikan,

The Rt. Rev. Prof. Akao- my Old Testament and Hebrew Lecturer. Also The Rt. Rev. Dr. Bayo Obijole another New Testament lecturer who supervised my first Degree project: those men showed me love and concern as a student.

I must thank God also for the late Rev. FR. Professor J. Kennedy a lecturer of the Department of Religious studies Ibadan through whom I got access to the Library of the Dominican Institute, Ibadan – (May his soul Rest in Peace).

I must appreciate most sincerely some of my mentors and friends who have affected my life and ministry positively in particularly the Most Rev. Dr. Emmanuel Olisa Chukwuma OON; and his wife Dr. Mrs. Joyce Chukwuma who have kept me close since my days from Immanuel College Ibadan. The Most Rev. Dr. & Mrs. Caleb Amy Maduoma, who have demonstrated parental concern, then my friend and class mate in school – The Rt. Rev. and Mrs. G.N. Chukwukwunenye. These people's love is unquantifiable, may the Lord bless them richly.

I must not fail to acknowledge the love of some of the congregations which I have ministered to: St. Paul's Church, Oke-Bola, Ibadan, St. Thomas' Church, Isinkan, Akwe, All Saints' Church, Ijomu Akure, The Cathedral of the Good Shepherd, St. Paul's Church, Chinatown, Holy Spirit Chapel IMT & Holy Spirit Chapel ESUT Agbani, Emmanuel Church, Achara Layout and now All Saints' Church, G.R.A; Enugu. These people have been very loving and wonderful.

Mention must be made of the love I shared with the staff and students of the Good Shepherd Anglican seminary Enugu. When I served there as the Principal, it was a rewarding experience. I am sincerely grateful to those who in one way or the other contributed to the success of this work especially in typing the manuscript proof reading and correcting errors.

I acknowledge with gratitude, the good works done by the authors of the books, articles and reports that I consulted. In the same vein, I thank the Rt. Rev. G.O. Olajde, the retired Bishop of Anglican Diocese of Ibadan, and the Ven. Chris

Okeke. Retired General Secretary of scripture Union (Nig) for their audience for interviews, and all others from whom I received information in regard to this book.

I am highly indebted to my wife Mrs. Obiageli G. Gad-Nwosu and my children, Charis, Ugochukwu, Joshua, Favour and Marvelous for their love, prayers and support, they are blessed.

May the good Lord grant that we all prosper and have in abundance and be freed from the disease of poverty, for Jesus Christ's sake. Amen.

Jesus' Attitude to Wealth and Poverty

INTRODUCTION

"Every human being would like to satisfy himself with the good things of this world". This desire ought to be put under reasonable control. It would be good if "the good things" is quest or desire to improve the social well-being of mankind. It could also be good if it is a desire to get sufficient things which is in keeping with one's position in life.

Nevertheless, it is sad that human beings find it difficult to put their material urge in check within reasonable limits. There is often the temptation to covet or steal what belongs to others, or to deprive others their right. This type of temptation comes to people in so many subtle forms and often times get rooted in a person. This is dangerous for a harmonious living in the society. Something must be done urgently to put desires for "good things" under control.

Someone may wish to be great and powerful among men and then be tempted to grind down his workers' wages and cheat customers. One also may seek for an ever increasing comfort and thereby be tempted to fill the boot of his car with ill-gotten money from his employer or government as some Nigerian politicians do; or like a sort of "Robin Hood', one may desire to help the poor beyond his means and then be tempted to increase his income unlawfully by investing in an unlawful but lucrative business like drug pushing, smuggling of petrol or bunkering, '419', etc. It may also be that one is just a selfish human being, who is greedy and dishonourable. Such people care not about the right and welfare of others. Their determined policy may just be to acquire wealth either by hook or crook with the one proviso that they do not get gaoled in the process.

One could as well be among those who shunned this temptation, or may be one of the few in the society who are eaten up with the desire for justice to the poor. Who would want charity to be increased upon the poor to whom a lot of injustices are being mete out. It is to this group of people that every Christian ought to belong.

"This desire for an ever-rising standard of life is not just cupidity" as L.S. Hunter puts it,[1] but what are we going to do about it? How does it stand in relation to the teachings of our Lord, "Be not anxious for meat, drink and raiment" (Luke 12:22), and to His assurance "seek you first the kingdom of God, and all these things shall be added unto you". (Luke 12:31)? What must Christians do to control unrighteous

1. Leslie Hunter, The Seed and the Fruit, S.C.M. Press, London, 1951, p.67

desires, and balance the gap between the rich and the poor? Most preaching today about wealth do not come to grips with the way in which mammon has turned itself into a fairy 'godmother' and a universal 'aunt', or with the new tension and unrest in our social life which are arising as a result of it.

Canon A.E. Simpson remarks that modern society believes in money as the supreme good, and organizes itself for the acquisition of more and more money. That wealth is the idol which commands the homage of the world today, and the desire for wealth is responsible for most of the present troubles of the world. He quotes, "Little children, keep yourselves from idols" (1 John 5:21), and concludes, "There is no more relevant text in the Bible than this"[2]. Simpson has given us insight to the position wealth has occupied in the hearts of many Christians today. There is this insane thirst for riches today as an end in itself. The Church tends to also have been encouraging this.

Staurt Briscoe[3] as is quoted by Gregory Lewis, says:

> *"Much of the emphasis in American evangelical Christianity is: if you came to Jesus, he'll give you all you want and he'll make you successful. That isn't the Christian Gospel. What Christ actually offered was: "If you're going to be my disciples, deny yourself and take up your cross".*

2. A.E. Simpson, "The Idolatry of Wealth", <u>The Rebel Church</u> (ed.) A.D. Belden et al, James Clarke and Company, London, p.90.

3. Gregory Lewis, <u>Is God for Sale?</u>, Tyndale House: Illinois, 1979, P.13

One would see from Briscoe's point here that some evangelicals seem to measure faith by wealth and success.

There is a major issue with many Christian believers today, and that is trying to make sure they enjoy the best of the two worlds. "God is a realistic God; He knows our minds like nobody else does or ever will (Psalm 139). He knows that we want so much to have him, but also to have the world; He knows that we want the security of world's goods at the same time"[4].

We are living now in an age which could be regarded as "affluent age". It could also be regarded as "technological age" "the Jet age". Barclays, quoting F.R. Barry, says that for the majority of Christians, the call is to the sanctification of wealth. Also quoting Briank Rice he writes "Affluence in the hands of fallen man is a double-edged blessing and the source of much evil"[5].

A new trend in modern life has been brought in by the availability of facilities and recourses to many which hitherto was not so. They were available in the past to only a relative few individuals or places. As a result of scientific discoveries and new industrial revolutions, there is now a range of interesting things, amusements, activities and material possessions to the level that were not known before now. What matters today is cash; there are a lot of things to buy, both for luxury and necessity. However, unless one has the purchasing power, life can become miserable and a lonely affair. For this

4.   Ibid., P. 24

5.   William Barclay, Ethics in a Permissive Society Fount Paperbacks, Glassgow, 1984, P. 143.

reason, everyone wants money at all cost, and more and more of it. Today, the Nigerian society seems to know nothing, but money and to get it no matter how. Money seems to be the basis for everything in Nigeria. The Church is not out of this either.

According to Andrew Kirk:

"The real scandal of the poor in the world today is not only their poverty and the misery it creates, but the ostentatious affluence of the rich. Our moral credulity is stretched to breaking point by those who want to find reasons for justifying the incredible difference in lifestyle existing between the poor majority of almost every nation"[6]

Wealth has been noted as the main idol of modern mind.[7]

It is not my intention in this book, to condemn wealth and promote poverty as a virtue. There is actually nothing wrong for a man to want to earn enough money to keep himself and his family in reasonable comfort, and to provide for the future but that is quite different from the neglect of the poor and seeing poverty as a deadly disease cause by sin, and enthroning wealth in the mind as the supreme good for human life. This gives the impression that the poor is hell bound while the rich is already in the kingdom of heaven. Wealth is not evil

6. Andrew Kirk, <u>A New World Coming</u>, Marshalls: London, 1983, P.60.
7. A.E. Simpson, <u>op.cit.,</u> P.93

but the worship of it. There are sections of the society where it is accepted that the highest goal for any boy is to become a millionaire. This could be true of Nigeria.

What was Jesus' attitude to wealth and poverty and what implication has this for the Christians in Nigeria?

1

WEALTH

1.1 THE CONCEPT OF WEALTH

As in the Interpreter's Dictionary of the Bible, there are two Hebrew words "hawan" and "hayal" which are translated 'wealth'. These words originally mean 'faculty", "ability" or power[8]. Wealth by this means the observable and tangible evidence of the ability to acquire possession, and the power that gives over others.

From the above idea, we can see with Canon Simpson[9] that great wealth means power, power over the lives and fortunes of men, power to influence policies of nations. It is this power which much wealth puts into the hands of small group of persons that is the dangerous thing. And when this power is used, as it must be, for the private interest of those

8. F.W. Young, "Wealth" The Interpreter's Dictionary of the Bible, Vol.4 (ed.) George Arthur Buttrick, Abingdon Press, London, 1962, pp.818-819.

9. A.E. Simpson, op.cit., P.94.

possessing it, the danger is all the more, greater. It is the power that wealth brings that is the most attractive thing in it. It is power and ability that people really crave for.

In the Greek Old Testament version, various Hebrew words are translated by <u>Ploutos</u>. The word-group connected with this is found thirty-two times in the historical books, thirty-four times in the prophets, sixteen times in the Psalms, and ninety-three times in the Wisdom literature. It follows from this summary that it was chiefly the teachers of wisdom of the post-exilic period who were pre-occupied with the question of wealth and riches[10].

In the King James Version of the Bible, the word 'goods', riches', 'substance', 'stuff', 'vessels', 'to take spoil', 'carriage', 'office', is used to mean wealth. In the New English Bible it is referred to as herds, property, possessions, chattels, treasure, wealth, etc. These meaning material possessions of various kinds often used of that which is plundered, stolen, or confiscated. Both Hebrew '<u>hon'</u> (occurring only in poetry) and 'hail' speak of wealth in general. Except for Proverbs 6:31, all of the above-mentioned occurrences of these two words concern the seizure or plunder of such wealth. Hebrew '<u>rekus'</u> is a general term for possessions. Similarly, Hebrew <u>Keli</u> and Hebrew <u>Melaka</u> are general terms for possessions, with some overlap in meaning apparent in Exodus 22:7f., Hebrew <u>Manasseh</u>, probably refers to man-made or processed goods of all kinds.

28

10. Robert Koch, "Riches", <u>Encylopedia of Biblical</u> Theology, Vol. II (ed.) J.B. Bauer: Sheed and Ward, London, 1970,pp.775-780.

In the New Testament, the meanings of the words are more obvious. Four Greek words speak of "possession". Greek word Tasa (Lit. "What is your"), ta hyparchonta, and hyparxis ('what one has'), as well as Katecho ('to possesses'). Greek word dios referring to earthly life or manner of life, emphasizes the "Meaning of Living" generally on a subsistence level (cf. Mark 12:44, Luke 8:43). Another Greek word is porphyropolis which means a dealer in purple fabrics or goods (Acts 16:14)[11]. The rich man in the parable of Lazarus was said to have dressed in purple – a sign of wealth.

Money is another important factor in wealth. According to the Encyclopedia of Religion and Ethics, it is the name applied to the instrument devised by man which enables him conveniently to effect exchange of goods and services. It was a great advance upon Carter when an intermediary was adopted by the traffic – King parlies Ibrat provided at a generally acceptable medium of exchange[12].

There are six Greek words which are rendered 'money' in various English versions of the New Testament. These are argursion (Matthew 25:18, 27, 28:12, 15, mark 14:11, Luke 9:3, 19:15, 23, 22:5); Chalkos (Mark 6:8, 12:41), kerma (John 2:15), nomisma (Matthew 22:19) ta didrachma (Matthew 17:24)[13].

Money plays a prominent role in determining wealth. Gregory Lewis states that money is the chief means that the world has for satisfying its desires. That the main mental and

---

11. Lee Gary A., "Goods" International Standard Bible Encyclopedia, vol. II (ed.) Geoffrey W. Bromiley et al., William B. Erdmans Publishing, England, 1982, P. 528.

12. A.B.D. Alexander, :"Wealth" Encyclopaediaof Religion and Ethics, Vol.12, (ed). James Hasting, T. and Y. Clark, Edinburgh, 1958, P. 720.

13. Dictionary of Christ and the Gospel Vol. 4 (ed.) James Hasting, T. and T. Clarke, Edinburgh.

emotional advantage of having money is that it gives one, not only sense of well-being, but a sense of power, of control, to him money touches man's daily existence materially, emotionally and socially[14].

Another factor in wealth is property. According to Cassells English Dictionary[15,] property is peculiar or inherent quality, character, nature, that which is owned, a possession or possessions, an estate, exclusive right of possession, ownership.

Property has a social as well as an individual aspect and the right to it is not absolute but conditional. The right of private ownership can be limited by the state, but only in so far as the needs of the community require this. Like the property regulation right of Obasanjo regime in Nigeria in 1978[16].

As for the exercise of the ownership right, or the use of property, divine and natural law impose upon owners (who are no more than stewards of such before God to whom account must be given), responsibilities in regard to the community. Serious sin can be committed by not providing for one's family, by paying unjust wages, by investing money with a view only to profit without regard to the effects and nature of goods produced, and by sheer extravagance when many are in need[17]. The legitimacy of private property is affirmed throughout the Bible. God wants only a fair distribution of his natural endowment.

30

14.   Gregory Lewis, op.cit., P. 95
15.   A.L. Hayward, "Money" Cassells English Dictionary (ed) J.J. Sparkes, Cassells, London, 1979.
16.   Land use Decree, 1978 in Official Gazette, vol. 65, No.14, 29th March, 1978, Part A Paragraph 62.
17.   Andrew Gordon, S.J., Security, Freedom and Happiness, Catholic Social Guild, Oxford, 1944, P. 116.

Wealth consists also of things which are immaterial; someone's natural endowment or knowledge which some regard as "talent" could be regarded as wealth. It could mean spiritual height. When one is filled with the Holy Spirit, he could be regarded as spiritually wealthy; spiritual wealth means being in total friendly relationship with God. This idea is meant in the third letter of John verse two.

WEALTH CREATION

Wealth could be created through investments in business, through borrowing, through labour and wages through stealing, fraud, gambling and exportations, looting or through accomplishment in life which attracts reward in cash or kind. Wealth could be said to be created through any economic activities of man, for that is what economics is all about.

WEALTH DISTRIBUTION

Right from the Old Testament, we see how God wanted his people to administer wealth distribution. This could be noticed in the Jubilee Principle[18] in Leviticus 25. This is one of the most radical texts of the Bible with regard to wealth distribution, at least for people born in countries committed to Laissez-faire economics. God demanded that all lands must be returned to the original owners every fifty years. (Leviticus

18. Ronald J. Sider, The Rich Christians in an age of Hunger, Paulist Press, New York, 1977, P. 88

25:10-24). God demands economic justice for his people. We shall discuss this further in chapter two.

1.2   THE CONCEPT OF POVERTY

Poverty according to Yves Congar O.P. can be considered as a simple economic fact, that is, the position of the 'have not', the situation of deprivation.   Here we can distinguish several degrees of poverty which are not merely a matter of quantity. In the domain of possibilities and human development, quantitative degrees easily become qualitative differences. According to Pope Pious XII, poverty is the living space.

Following the French Jurist, J. Hamel, we may distinguish four degrees of poverty which are:

(1)   Misery, or the situation of those who do not have enough to provide for those necessary needs of man;

(2)   It could be the extreme opposite of richness or 'the situation of those who, within their environment, possess an abundance of goods, allowing them to indulge in all the superfluities of their liking to a very large extent.

(3)   The opposite of also the well-to-do, who have 'enough wealth to achieve an average affluence compared with others   of   their   environment,   but   without   appreciable superfluity' (a relative position), and

(4)   Poverty, or 'the situation of those who cannot manage to achieve the common standard of their environment and who, without lacking the essentials, must deny themselves certain satisfactions that appear normal to those among whom they are living[19].

The word poverty is the state of being poor. So further to that concept, let us know what is meant by 'the poor'. In the Bible the Greek word <u>Ptochos</u> is translated by the A.V. as 'poor'. There is still a deep meaning in this Greek word '<u>ptochos</u>'. There is another word in Greek translated 'poor' that is <u>penes</u>, which simply describes the man for whom life and living is a struggle, the man who is the reverse of the man who lives in affluence. <u>Ptochos</u> on its own comes from the verb <u>ptossein</u>, which means to cower or crouch, and it describes not simply honest poverty, and the struggle of the labouring man to make ends meet, it describes abject poverty, which has literally nothing and which is in imminent danger of real starvation. <u>Ptochos</u> does not describe gentle poverty, but real, acute destitution.

There are two Hebrew words behind this Greek word <u>Ptochos</u> these are <u>ebion</u> and <u>ani</u>. The meanings of two words developed in three stages, first: the words simply mean 'poor' in the sense of lacking in this word's goods (Deut. 15:4, 11). Second; they go on to mean since, 'poor' then 'downtrodden and oppressed' (Amos 2:6, 8:4). Third; the two above meanings put together, gives the fact that, if a man is poor and downtrodden and oppressed, he has no influence on earth, no power and no prestige. Therefore in William Barclay's

33

19. Franze Bockle, <u>War, Poverty, Freedom, Vol. 15,</u> Paulist Press, New York, P. 49

words, "He cannot look to men for help and when all help and resources of earth are closed to him, he can only look to God"[20]. Therefore, these words come to describe people who, because they have nothing on earth, have come to put their absolute hope and total trust in God. (Amos 5:12, Psalm 10:2, 12, 17, 12:5, 14:6, 68:10).

William I. Byron, S.I.[21] describes poverty as the 'sustained deprivation of wealth (and, derivatively, deprivation of health, shelter, food, education, employment and human dignity)". Poverty to him is maintained by social and political power, exercised in a frame-work of human relationships. This power resides in a combination of three factors, numbers, resources, and organization. The poor out-number the affluent, but the affluent have resources and organization. The status of being affluent or poor is re-enforced by law, social custom and values, and direct or indirect control of police and military power by the affluent. The poor unwillingly support the power that keeps them poor.

Poverty, for Marxist theory, is distinguished from ethical or certain religious notions in that it is not a normal problem. Marxists do not criticize or cure poverty because it contradicts a normal idea or a principle of justice. The circumstance of the distribution of poverty and riches is a historical result, the consequence of human action, and therefore something which is essentially changeable. Therefore that distribution of poor and rich does not depend much on

34

20. William Barclay, New Testament Words, S.C.M. Press London, 1976, P. 248.

21. William J. Byron, "Poverty" The Earth is the Lords (ed.) Mary Evelyn Jegen and Brunov, Manno, Paulist Press, New York, 1978, P. 150.

natural factors but on the actual form of the society. So long as production occurs under strict condition of scarcity, domination is unavoidable. But in the era of capitalist production stringency seems to be at an end; riches for all seem possible and domination seems superfluous. Marx did not though stop at these general presuppositions, but tried to delineate the capitalist dynamics of self-surpassing progress. This ultimately is dependent upon the contradiction of capital and labour. Its main aim is the transition from private control of the means of production to social control. That would remove the antagonism of property-owing and impoverished classes, and solve the problem of poverty. Hence poverty is not a natural category but something that can be determined only within the context of whatever wealth are possible historically within particular circumstances.

In Marx theory of labour values, he develops the notion that the proletarian sells his only means of production which is labour in order to live and receives wages, usually based on the market price, whereas the capitalist earns more from the work force more than what it causes him in wages. Then what it means is that the work force becomes poorer. Hence riches depend on the exploitation of the work force which is usually the poor[22].

Coenraad Boerma reported that the 1983 report by the Ecumenical Commission for Church and Society of the European Community (ECCS) in Brussels pointed out that any

35

22. Werner Post, "The Poor" Ibid., P. 75

attempt to define poverty is not only risky, but also elitist and that the best way to come to an understanding of poverty is to ask the people themselves (i.e the poor) what they understand by the word. This was done by them in Great Britain through a survey, from which a list was compiled of those conditions deemed necessary for a human existence. The result seemed to have shown that poverty must first be understood in a rational context. Poverty then is to be seen as dynamic and not static. Poverty naturally has to do with the basic necessities of life (food, shelter, clothing), but also with total illiteracy. Nevertheless, it above all, has to do with the manner of participating in the culture and society to which one belongs. Poverty is the inability for one to take advantage of the opportunities which society offers. It is being shut out, having no power, no choice to make in the possibilities and conflicts that make up the society[23].

According to Hubert Lepargneur[24] poverty is people experiencing the lack of the necessities of life, and the necessary means to acquire them. One in such a situation is experiencing being poor. Poverty as a human phenomenon can be defined as powerlessness, incapacity. It can be contrasted with other socio-economic states, but also includes a strong psychological element. As the powerful tend to relate to each other, notably by infiltration and exchange, poverty emerges; the poor are not poor of their own free-will.

This negative definition according to him (Hubert) also

23. Coenraad Boerma, The Poor Side of Europe, WCC, Geneva, 1989,P. 4.
24. Hubert Lepargneur, "The problem of Poverty and How the Church can help", The Poor and the Church (ed) Nosbert Greinecher and Alois Muller, Cross Road Books, New York, 1977, P.89.

has a positive aspect, that is, that poverty includes hope of making real progress. Poverty is the dynamic of the process of liberation like 'necessity' they say 'is the mother of invention'. Wretched conditions of life are merely a weight, crushing the spirit. Poverty, which apart from the fact that it may most of the time be regarded as temporary, is compatible, even connected with freedom of the spirit, warmth of heart, the health of the soul and spiritual joy. So the positive aspect of poverty is often connected to the concept of freedom, that freedom from the obsession with wealth and the slavery of the grinding need.

Poverty is made up of different categories which are material, spiritual and voluntary. Material poverty includes the lack of the necessities of life, like food, shelter, clothing, education, etc. Material poverty is a wide-spread phenomenon. It is the most significant aspect of poverty.

Spiritual poverty is the opposite of material poverty. Some have regarded this kind of poverty as theological which is seen as the authentic Christian poverty[25]. This is the poverty according to the pattern wrought in the human spirit by Jesus' example and gift. It is an essential articulation of faith as obediential hearing, which allows one to step out of the narrow space of self-definition into God's immense freedom. In this poverty, one does not even cling to his virtue as a possession. According to Luke T. Johnson, "To accept our worth from God as a gift means to dwell in continual

37

25. L.J. Johnson, <u>Sharing Possessions, Mandate and Symbol of Faith</u>, Fortress Press, Philadelphia, 1981, P.80

nakedness before him, in the most radical form of poverty[26]. We shall discuss more on this as we discuss Jesus' attitude to wealth and poverty.

CREATION OF POVERTY

Poverty could be created by forces which are both external and internal. The external forces could be those inflicted by the societal setting or natural causes such as war, economic imbalance, alienation, population growth[27] while the internal forces are those which the people inflict upon themselves through their attitude to life. Some of these are: attitude to work which includes laziness, unfaithfulness, truancy, etc. Others are: inferiority complex, fear of failure, extravagancy, and gluttony of over-indulgence.

WHO ARE THE POOR

A poor man could mean someone so destitute that he has to beg. It could also be someone who, for various reasons, cannot get along without help. His situation may be due to precariousness or to lack of financial resources, to being without the food, clothing or lodging needed for survival, to physical or mental handicap, to loss of liberty, to lack of education, or to having no satisfying human contact.

He is one who has no prestige or honour. The word 'poor' can be extended to cover all the oppressed, all those who are dependent upon the mercy of others and all those

26. Ibid
27. Ronald J. Sider, Christ and Violence, Herald Press, Canada, 1979.

who rely entirely upon God's mercy[28]. In fact, to be poor could not be a virtue or desirable.

28. Robert L. Stivers, <u>Hunger, Technology and Limits to Growth</u>, Ausburg Publishing House, A Minneopolis, 1984, pp. 22, 24, and 26

2

THE OLD TESTAMENT IDEA

OF WEALTH AND POVERTY

I choose to write this chapter in order to enable us have a working knowledge of what the idea was before the time of Jesus. This is necessary because most of Jesus' teachings are based upon the Old Testament. This was the scripture before His incarnation. He also claimed to be fulfilling the law and the prophets. He had no mission of abolishing the established codes; so let us first discuss wealth in the Old Testament.

2.1   WEALTH IN THE OLD TESTAMENT

There are in the Old Testament a lot of materials in relation to wealth. In the Old Testament wealth is regarded as a blessing and a reward for godliness. A good man in the Old Testament flourishes and prospers, unlike the New Testament, which tends to see the good man as afflicted and in trouble. There is a strong line of idea in the Old Testament which seems to link prosperity with goodness and adversity with wickedness. A good example is Job's comforters. (Job 4:7). We note significantly that after Job's affliction, he finished up with renewed and increased prosperity. (Job 42:10-17)[1]. Job's example also shows that the righteous do suffer, like in the case of the suffering servant of Isaiah 53, 3; Job 1:8.

Prosperity was interpreted highly as God's blessing, and reward for fidelity. For example, the Palmist said, "I have been young and now am old, yet I have not seen the righteous forsaken, or his children begging bread". (Psalm 37:25). Also the fear of the Lord is said to give man wealth and riches (Psalm 112, 1-3). This in fact is the idea that runs through most of the passages in the wisdom literature where Wealth is discussed. Proverbs 10:32 says, "The blessing of the Lord makes rich, and he adds no sorrow with it". Wisdom is said to have long life in her right hand, and honour and riches in her left. Riches and honour are with her, also with lasting wealth and prosperity (Proverbs 3:16, 8:18).

There is another line of thought in Proverbs which tends to take a middle stand in relation to wealth. This sees the way of happiness as having neither too much nor too little. One of the wise men Agur prays with an impulse of godly fear

1. William Barclay, <u>Ethics in a Permissive Society.</u> Fount Paperbacks, Glassgow, 1984. P.147

and trembling, saying, "Give me neither poverty nor riches; feed me with food that is needful for me. Lest I be full and deny thee, and say, "Who is the Lord? or lest I be poor, and steal, and profane the name of my God (Proverb 30:8,9). This implies, not a bare sufficiency for natural life, but a provision varying according to the calling, in which God has placed one[2]. This is very much in line with certain Greek doctrine of the happy medium – "The golden mean". And this seems to have been recommended by the Patriarchs (Genesis 28:20), and the Prophets (Jeremiah 45:5).

The Old Testament emphasizes that prosperity is a gift from God. The preacher felt it should be enjoyed as that (Ecclesiastes 5:19). But this does not fall to man without personal effort for "A slack hand causes poverty, but the hand of the diligent makes rich". (Proverb 10:4). The Old Testament sees wealth as giving a sort of security to the possessor. "A rich man's wealth is his strong city, and like a high wall protecting him" (Proverbs 18:11, 10:15). Nevertheless, there is inadequacy in wealth. "The righteous man will flourish, but the man who trusts in riches will wither". (Proverbs 11:28). It is not a substitute for character and goodness. If riches increase, one must not set his heart on them. (Psalm 62:10). Riches are temporary things, which do not last forever. (Proverbs 27:4). Wealth at its best is a secondary good. A good name is to be chosen in place of great riches, and favour is better than silver or gold (Proverbs 22:1). And "Better is a

2.   George F. Santa, A Modern Study in the Rock of Proverbs, Mott Media, Milford, USA., 1978, P. 706

little that the righteous man has than the abundance of many wicked (Psalm 37:16)[3].

There are other passages of the wisdom literatures which depict wealth as of a secondary good. It may not allow one sound sleep (Ecclesiastes 5:12). To concentrate everything in search of wealth is short-sightedness (Proverbs 28:22). No man carries wealth away when he dies (Psalm 49:16, Job 1:21, Ecclesiastes 5:15, 16). It is something that cannot be relied upon (Proverbs 23:4,5). Wealth in certain cases could be a hindrance instead of a help[4] (Ecclesiastes 5:13, Jeremiah 17:11, 73:12, Psalm 52:7).

In the Old Testament, private property ownership is sanctioned by God. The Ten Commandments enjoined this implicitly and explicitly. God forbids stealing and covetousness (Exodus 20:15, 17, Deuteronomy 5:19, 21).

This right in any case is not absolute. In the Old Testament view point, property owners are not free to seek their own profit in disregard to needs of fairer economics of their neighbours. They must love their neighbours as themselves. This is contrary to the laissez –faire belief that the right of private property is absolute and inviolable. In the Old Testament, God is the only absolute owner, for "the earth is the Lord's and the fullness thereof, the world and those who dwell therein." (Psalm 24:1). The Old Testament still maintains that right to property is in subordination to the obligation to care for the weaker members of the society[5].

3.   William Barclay, op.cit., P. 148
4.   Ibid., P. 149
5.   Ronald J. Sider, The Rich Christians in the Age of Hunger, Paulist Press New York, 1977, PP. 113-114.

The Old Testament enjoins economic justice. That is why we have that radical passage of Leviticus 25. Land in Israel was capital and the basic means of production, Israel being an agricultural community. At the beginning of Israel as a nation after the settlement, land was (sort of) divided equally among the tribes and families with the exception of the Levites who were to have the Lord's portion. Apparently, God wished this basic economic equality to continue hence he commanded the return of all lands to the original owners after fifty years. The people do not then sell land, but lease it. This is so because Yahweh is the owner of all land and human beings are only stewards (Leviticus 25:23).

In order to further make sure that the interest of the underprivileged is protected; God also declared for the people: "The Sabbatical Year". This is every seventh year when (according to the law) soil, slaves and debtors will be liberated. In fact, a debt after seven years would not be required by the creditor. Hebrew slaves at this sabbatical year received their freedom and will not go empty handed (Exodus 23:10-18, Leviticus 25:2-7, Deuteronomy 15:12-18, Exodus 21:2-6, cf Deuteronomy 15:1-6, 9, 10). The main issue behind this law is God's concern for justice to the poor and the disadvantaged.

In verse 4 of Deuteronomy 15, we could see that God promised the people that there would be no poor among them in the land, and that is on the condition of their obedience to the principles of wealth distribution which he set for them. But for the fact they would disobey, God said in verse 11, that the poor would not cease in the land. God still commanded them to open up their hands to them. God went further to set before them, the law of tithing and gleaning, in order to protect the poor and even his servants – the Levites (who have no portion (Deuteronomy 14:28-29, Leviticus 17:30-33, Deuteronomy 26:12-15, Numbers 18:21-32). It was this law of gleaning that helped the widow Ruth to survive (Ruth 2)[6].

The Old Testament writers know that wealth is a blessing from God, still they know that it can separate a man from God and from his fellow men. They also know that wealth is a good thing to be enjoyed, and yet a bad thing for man to rely upon or to give his life in pursuit. Having discussed wealth in the Old Testament, let us now see poverty in the Old Testament.

2.2   POVERTY IN THE OLD TESTAMENT

Poverty, we note, is the state of being poor. In the Old Testament there are three words used which are: (a) dal meaning one who is poor and weak and even emaciated. This is the word used for the lean cattle in Pharaoh's dream (Genesis 41:19). (b) ebion which the Revised Standard Version regularly translates need (Job 5:15, Psalm 69:33, etc). The word expresses the man whose poverty has brought oppression and abuse to him. (c) 'ani and anaw', which describes the man

6. Ibid., P. 92

46

who is poor, without influence, oppressed. One who has no human help and resources, but has only God to trust. That is the poor and humble man, whose whole trust is in God (Psalm 34:6, 40:17)[7].

It is laid in the Old Testament a special duty to help and care for the poor. One who remembers the poor is said to be happy (Psalm 41:1, proverbs 14:21). To show oneself as a good man, one must maintain the right of the poor and needy (Proverbs 31:9, Job 34:19). The ideal ruler would be expected to safeguard the rights of the poor (Isaiah 11:3-5). God commanded that justice must be given to the weak and the fatherless, and the right of the afflicted and the destitute must be maintained. Further, he commanded the rescue of the weak and the needy, and their deliverance from the hand of the wicked (Psalm 82:3,4). So the Old Testament sees it as an essential part of a good man's duty to remember, to help and to defend the poor.

There is constant condemnation in the Old Testament, of those who neglect or mal-treat the poor as being evil. (Psalm 10:2, Isaiah 3:14, 15, 10:1-2, 32:7, Proverbs 22:16, 29:7). The sense of justice, grounded in Yahweh's own concern for the poor induced the prophets to denounce all wealth gained at the expense of the poor (e.g Amos 2:6-7, Isaiah 3:13-24, Jeremiah 6:26-29, Micah 2:1-2). The prophets' protect us grounded in the same conviction as the simple reward – punishments scheme – that Yahweh rewards rectitude and

7. William Barclay, op.cit, P. 150

punishes injustice. Obadiah 24 is a poignant portrait of the exploited poor. Such wealth used in oppression of the poor would be destroyed by God in his justice[8].

The Old Testament also laid the care of the poor down as a duty to God. It is something that has to be done also for the sake of God. To judge the cause of the poor and the needy would mean the knowledge of God of a good king as stated by Jeremiah (Jeremiah 22:16). To oppress the poor is to insult his maker- God, but to be kind to the needy means honouring God (Proverbs 14:31). Kindness to the poor also means lending to God (Proverbs 19:17). For God to hear one's cry, one must hear that of the poor (Proverbs 21:13). God will plead the cause of the poor and despoil the life of those who despoil them (Proverbs 22:23).

The Old Testament shows then that God has special concern for the poor. He hears them (Psalm 69:33). He stands at the right hand of the needy (Psalm 109:31). He would not forget them and their hope shall never perish (Psalm 9:18). He provides for them in his kindness (psalm 68:10). He raises the poor up from the dust (1 Samuel 2:8) and gives justice to the poor with righteousness (Isaiah 11:4)[9]. So the poor man is under the total care of the Lord.

From the above treatment of the Old Testament idea of wealth and poverty, we could observe that the Old Testament does not despise wealth; it does not reject the benefits of wealth. But it has never made wealth the principal good. It

8. L.E. Keck, "Poor" The Interpreter's Dictionary of the Bible, Supplementary Vol. (ed.) Keith Crim, Abingdon Nashville 1976, P. 673.
9. William Barclay, op.cit., P. 152

also insisted that to gain wealth wrongly and to use it in disregard of true stewardship are evil and offence against God. It also maintained a privileged position of the poor in relation to God. This being the foundation upon which Jesus built his attitude to wealth and poverty. We shall discuss this Jesus' attitude in the next chapter.

3

JESUS' ATTITUDE TO WEALTH AND POVERTY

This chapter shall be concentrated on Jesus' teaching and response to Wealth and Poverty. We shall start with these teachings as they are depicted in the parable of Jesus.

3.1   WEALTH AND POVERTY IN THE PARABLES OF JESUS

This sub-heading tends from the fact that most of the sayings and teachings of Jesus are through parables. In fact, going through the gospels one could discover that almost all his attitude to wealth are expressed in parables. So for our true understanding of his true position, it would be better to discuss these parables one after the other. Parable has been defined as a comparison drawn from nature or daily life and designed to illuminate some spiritual truth, on the assumption that what is valid in one sphere is valid as well in the other. It is a form of teaching.

The word parabole, is Greek word which means a comparison or analogy. The antecedents of Christ's parable must be sought in Israel not in Hellas, in the Old Testament Prophets and the Jewish Fathers not in the Greek orators. Doubtless, Jesus learnt the use of Parables[1]. Therefore parables are important in conveying most of his messages. Let us now see those which teach on the above subject.

(a) The Steward: (Matthew 24:45-51, Luke 12:42-46). Matthew and Luke follow the parable of the thief with that of the steward. This is one of the five parables of the parousia[2]. The master here talks of a servant or steward to be relied upon, who would not be an eye-server. This could be lesson for a good working ethics. This parable shows that those who are employed to work must not behave any way they like or play truancy at work.

(b) The Talents and the Pounds: (Matthew 25:14-30, Luke 19:11-27). The key word in this parable is reliability[3]. The parable describes how the master entrusts his wealth to his servants "according to their ability" – (a talent is a weight, which later became a large unit of money), and how the first two servants set to work and doubled the money entrusted to

52

1.   A.M. Hunter, Interpreting the Parables, SCM Press Limited, London, 1981, P.8
2.   Michael Green, Matthew for Today, Hodder and Stoughton London, 1988, P. 238.
3.   Ibid., P. 240

them. The third digs a hole and hides the money in the ground – that is, a recognized way of preserving something, and a guaranteed way of not increasing it. The master returns after a long time and called for account. The first two received commendation from the master while the third was condemned.

This shows that when one is responsible in the management of few things, greater responsibilities would be committed into his hands. This parable focuses not on the unexpectedness of the time of the master's return, but on the responsibility and accountability of the servants. The parable underlines points made in the other parables above, but if the parable of the steward emphasizes the need for faithfulness as opposed to self-indulgence, this emphasizes the need for hard-work and productivity rather than laziness and timidity. It is a warning against sloth probably induced by unwillingness to take risks.[4] The man who hides his talent under the ground is reminiscent of the one who hides his lamp under the ground and that too is reminiscent of the one who hides his lamp under a jar when it ought to be used to give light (Matthew 5:15). And the taking of the talent from the lazy one and the giving of it to the one with ten talents is reminiscent of the saying about the measure one gives and gets (Mark 4:24).

In resemblance to Matthew's parable of the talents is that of Luke's parable of pounds or minas. In this, the servants are given money to trade with by a master when he goes

4.   Ibid, P. 241

away, two servants do very well and are rewarded with greater authority- they are put in-charge of cities. The third wrapped his money up and returned it unused, excusing himself by describing his master's harshness. Thus he was afraid because, according to him, "You (referring to his master) expect to get profit even when you have not invested, you expect to reap where you have not sown'. Consequently the angry master responded, "surely, then, you should have put the pound into a deposit account so that I could claim interest on it. Therefore he was deprived of the one he had. Both Matthew and Luke end the parable with Jesus saying, "To everyone who has, more will be given, but from the one who has nothing, even what he has will be taken away".

The difference in these parables could be for the fact Jesus told parables many times and in different forms and we may have here two of his variants on a theme. Or another possibility is that Luke has woven two parables together, one like Matthew's parable about the servants responsibility, the other about enemies of the aspiring King[5]. The main message of both parables is a teaching against laziness, and the need for hard-work.

(c) <u>The Parable of the Rich Fool:</u> (Luke 12:13-21) Here, Jesus being a Rabbi was asked to decide over a property dispute. This is between two brothers, probably the younger one was being deprived of his position of inheritance. But Jesus not being an ordained Rabbi refused to decide the case.

5.   David Wenham, <u>The Parables of Jesus: Pictures of Revolution,</u> Hodder and Stoughton, London, 1989, P. 85

Jesus, however, went to the root of the matter by warning against covetousness.

This parable would have been motivated by His personal knowledge of the man in question. The man's life expresses a fundamental wrong philosophy of life, according to which possessions are all that really matter. This parable takes up the thought of Jesus' ministry as being a challenge to the rich establishments. It is a potent reminder of the folly of living for this world's possessions. This parable illustrates the deceitfulness of wealth of which is spoken of in the parable of the sower. Their deceitfulness lies in their tendency to give people an illusory sense of security, to fill people's thought and horizons, and to stifle any interest in the mission of God. Jesus referred to the man as a fool whose life would be taken and his money would be of no use. Jesus concluded the story, "A man can amass wealth yet still be a pauper in the sight of God'. This parable is found only in Luke which frequently condemns wealth itself, whereas Matthew's gospel condemned the love of wealth, meaning an obsession[6].

However, we may immediately say that the parable does not imply that material things are wrong in themselves, but only when they become the focus and goal of life. The parable is a critique of 'all kinds of greed', because as Paul says in Ephesians 5:5, using the same Greek word, greed is idolatry (pleonektes).

6. E.V. and K.G. Barrel, St. Luke's Gospel, John Murray 1985, p. 105.

(d) <u>The Richman and Lazarus (Luke 16:19-31):</u>

This parable was probably addressed not to the scribes and Pharisees, but to the Sadducees[7] and forms Jesus' answer to their demand for a sign. The parable was probably based on a popular tale about a rich man and a poor man and the reversal of their fortunes in the next life[8]. It tells two parts: (a) The story proper (19-26) with its account of what befell Dives and Lazarus when they died, and (b) the epilogue (27-31), where the demand for a sign is refused.

The rich man lived as affluently as he dressed. The word <u>euphrainomenos</u> translated literally meaning something like 'enjoying himself brilliantly'. He lived for pleasure – his own pleasure. It does not appear to have bothered him that there was a poor man 'lying' at his gate; the Greek word <u>ebebleto</u> literally means someone 'thrown' down on the ground, suggesting that he was a cripple of some sort. Lazarus means "God helps". The rich man did not help but God did and both died. The rich man would have received a splendid burial while the poor man did not. But in the life beyond the tide turned in favour of the poor man, who is in bliss and blessedness, but the rich man suffers in agony and torture – and the situation could not be turned around.

This parable in effect is condemning irresponsibility, lack of awareness, lack of concern[9]. The trouble with the rich man was not cruelty as such, but he never noticed Lazarus. To him Lazarus was part of the landscape. He could simply care

56

7.   T.W. Manson, <u>The Teaching of Jesus</u>, Cambridge University Press, 1963, P. 207f.
8.   A.M. Hunter, <u>op.cit., p.83</u>
9.   William Barclay, <u>Ethics in a Permissive Society</u> Fount paper Back, Glassgow, 1984, P. 157

less about Lazarus. This parable is an illustration that man may be condemned not only for what he had done, but for what he had left undone. The condemnation is for the man who has money and who is quite unconcerned about those who do not have, for those without sense of responsibility to the less fortunate ones.

There are people who could spend in a meal more than what a cleaner earns in a whole month. There are people whose one time dressing alone are always more than what a Professor in the Nigerian University earns for a month. What of the flashy cars that people move along with? Some of these vehicles cost more than a local government's budget for a whole year.

Jesus attitude here is that no person or nation has a right to live in luxury while others live in poverty. There is need for us to remember that life does not end here, and what shall be the reward after this life.

(e) <u>The Unjust Steward: (Luke 16:1-13), and Laying up Treasure in Heaven, and places at Table (Matthew 6:19-21, Luke 12:32-34, 14 :7-14):</u>

The parable of the unjust steward takes us back again to the world of big business. This seems the strangest of all the parables of Jesus, the parable in which every character is a rogue. The parable is about a steward who was discovered to be dishonest hence was about to be dismissed. With this dismissal awaiting him, with his being about to lose his

57

comfort, he went to his master's debtors and made alterations in their favour. He recorded in each case less than what they owe. In this way he would expect these to receive him in their home after he loses his job. But when the master discovered, instead of being angry with him praised him for the wisdom in providing for his future.

We notice its ending: "And the Lord (kyrios) praised the unjust steward because he had acted wisely, for the sons of this world are wiser in their own generation than the sons of light". We take 'the Lord' to be Jesus, not the steward's master (Luke 16:8). What Jesus applauded was not the man's roguery, but his resourcefulness in a tight spot. A clever maneuver[10].

This is what Barley refers to as an extraordinary parable. It is so extraordinary that it is clear that by the time Luke recorded it, its original lesson was lost, because Luke attaches no fewer than four different lessons to it[11] – and all of them are relevant to the question of Jesus' attitude to wealth.

Luke attached to it the following lessons:

(a) That what Jesus means in saying that "the sons of this world are wiser in their own generation than the sons of light (Luke 16:8) is that he needs disciples who will show as much practical sense of God's business as worldlings do in theirs. It is indeed true that this would be a different world, and the Church would be a very different place, if Christians put as much time, thought and energy into the business of true

10. A.M. Hunter, op.cit, p. 67.
11. William Barclay, op.cit., P. 160

Christian life, as they do into making money, or even into leisure spending. If a Christian learns to put more astuteness into being the Christian he ought to be, as the worldly man puts into maintaining his measure of comfort, then he would be a fruitful Christian.

(b)　　　　The parable urges the disciples to make use of worldly wealth, so that when it fails, they may be received into the eternal habitations – that is, to prepare for the future. William Lillie says that this, whatever else it means teaches that money is to be used as a means, and not as an end in itself. So it tells us that money is meant to be used and not to be kept and that it must never be regarded as an end in itself, but always as a means to an end-and the end towards which it is a means will be all important.[12]

(c)　　　　Jesus went further to teach on faithfulness in management. He says, "He who is faithful in a very little is faithful also in much, and he who is dishonest in a very little is dishonest also in much. If then you have not been faithful in the unrighteous mammon, who will entrust to you the true riches? And if you have not been faithful in that which is another's, who will give you that which is your own? (Luke 16:10-12). This shows that the way in which a man acts as a steward of a little shows how he will act if he is entrusted with much riches. Therefore, if a man is a poor manager of money, he hardly will be committed with spiritual riches. If a man could not manage properly what has been entrusted to him,

12.　Ibid, P. 161

for which he would be asked to give account, no one would give him wealth of his own to use as it pleases him.

"The life a Christian lives, says Barclay W. in business is in its own way a preparation for eternal life[13].

(d) Another lesson we learn from this parable is that no one could possibly be committed to two masters, that is, God and wealth. God has absolute claim upon man and he demands absolute loyalty.

So this parable and that of laying up treasure in heaven, and places at the table, are just about proper use of worldly wealth. Jesus' teaching in these parables is then: "Invest in the work of God", by which he means literal investment. Just as the dedicated Marxist revolutionary is expected to commit himself and finance to the cause, in the same way Jesus expects his followers to be practically, and not just theoretically, committed to the exciting world-changing mission that he inaugurated.[14] This is what really happened in the early church in Jerusalem. When it is noted that 'all who believed were together and had all things in common, and they sold their possessions and goods and distributed them to all, as any had need" (Acts 2:44, 45 cf Acts 4:34) thereby following Jesus' charge in Luke 14:33, 12:33.

(e) <u>The Great Feast (Luke 14:16-24)</u>

This is another parable of Jesus which reflects Jesus' attitude to wealth and poverty. This is also given in Matthew 22:1-14. However, Luke's own is about Jesus, the poor and the

60

13. Ibid., P. 162
14. David Wenham, Op.cit. P. 108

rich. It is a comment on the fact that the well-heeled of Palestine in general tended to reject Jesus, but the poor and the marginalized of the society welcome him. Matthew's parable hints that the rejection of Jesus by the leaders of Israel was for materialistic reasons. Luke's parable makes it plain that that was the main reason. Luke's is a warning to the rich. The explanation by the rich for not honouring the invitation is given thus, "I have bought a field, and I must go out and see it; I pray you, have me excused", "I have bought five yoke of oxen, and I go to examine them; I pray you, have me excused, "I have married a wife, and therefore, I cannot come. It has been suggested that the excuses are obviously spurious and so deliberately insulting.[15]

In describing the excuses of the invitees, Jesus is diagnosing the generally negative response of the wealthy of his society to his ministry whether consciously or unconsciously, they were rejecting the invitation to join the Kingdom of God, because of pre-occupation with family and business commitments. This is what Jesus explains in this parable, and pointed out its insulting trait and the fatal consequences. The rich will find themselves shut out of the kingdom while their place would be taken.

The invitation then went to "the poor and maimed and blind and lame. These are probably beggars on the street. The parable is thus an explanation of what has been called the "bias to the poor"[16] in Jesus' ministry. Although, Jesus called

15. Ibid, p. 137
16. Ibid., P. 138

both the rich and the poor alike, yet it was true that his ministry was more welcomed by the poor and downtrodden of the society than by the wealthy. The ministry of Jesus was good news to the poor and those who are conscious of their need, but to the rich it was perceived indeed by them as bad news.

(f)   <u>The two debtors (Luke 7:41-50)</u>

This parable also shows Luke's particular interest in Jesus' ministry to the disadvantaged. Luke brought out this interest right from the beginning of his gospel. In his description of Jesus' infancy he referred to Mary's song, the "magnificant', in which she speaks of God scattering the proud, lifting up the humble, filling the hungry with good things, and sending the rich empty away (Luke 1:46-55). It comes out in his description of Jesus' programmatic sermon at Nazareth with its text from Isaiah 61, "The Spirit of the Lord is upon me, because he has anointed me to preach good news to the poor... (cf Luke 4:18-19). It came out clear in his version of the Beatitudes: "Blessed are you who are poor...woe to you who are rich (Luke 6:20, 24). This parable teaches about debt cancellation or the principle as it is stated in Leviticus 25. This parable could be read along with Matthew 18:23-35. Though what is depicted here is forgiveness, but what is involved in both are debt or money borrowed or owed. Therefore it is not out of place to say that Jesus wanted people to be humane to the poor or less fortunate.

(f)   The Sheep and the Goats (Matthew 25:31-46)

Before we leave this portion let us briefly see this parable which could be regarded as a parable of the end-time. The striking feature in this parable is the way the king (that is, the son of Man) identifies himself with the hungry, the thirsty, the stranger, the naked, the sick and the imprisoned. He speaks of them as 'my brothers' and explains to his surprised hearers, "Truly, I say to you, as you did it to one of the least of these my brethren, you did it to me". Many recent scholars have argued that Jesus is here identifying himself specifically with his disciples, not with the poor in general. It is argued that elsewhere in Matthew Jesus speaks of his disciples, and not others, as his 'brethren', and also of then as 'one of the least'. (Matthew 10:42, 12:50, 18:10), this is seen as a clue to the meaning of the phrases "one of the least of these my brethren". It has also been argued that elsewhere Jesus identifies himself with the disciples in a way that parallels the parable of the sheep and the goats. For example, in Matthew 10:42, we find a striking similar passage to the parable in context that is all about the disciples' mission: "And whosoever gives to one of these little ones even a cup of cold water because he is a disciple, truly, I say to you, he shall not lose his reward".

There is nothing in the parable that suggest that the poor and needy refereed to are specifically disciples, unless the words 'the least of these my brothers' are taken to mean that.

63

But the words by themselves are not a very obvious indication that it is specially Jesus' followers who are in mind. Within the parable they are enough natural way for the king to express his identification with even his least favoured citizen.[17]

The parable is seen as Jesus' classical statement on Christian social responsibility. It teaches us about works of charity to the poor, and that faith working by love is all in all in Christianity. Judgment will be based on our love to our neighbour as ourselves as defined in the parable of the good Samaritan – the needy.[18] According to Matthew Henry's commentary, the good works here described imply three things:

(1)   Self-denial, and contempt of the world; reckoning the things of the world no further good things, than as we are enabled to do good with them.

(2)   Love to our brethren which is the second great commandment, and

(3)   A believing regard to Jesus Christ. That which is here rewarded is the relieving of the poor for Christ's sake out of love to him. Jesus in this parable calls his followers to a caring community.

Let us here examine the Greek words that are significant in most of Jesus' parables. These are <u>oikonomos</u> (Luke 12:42, Matthew 25:14-30) and <u>oikonomia</u> (Luke 16:2). <u>Oikonomia</u> is the management of the <u>oikos</u> (that is stewardship), the sum total of movable goods, livestock and

17. Ibid, P. 90
18. See: William M. Fletcher, <u>The Second Greatest Commandment,</u> Navpress, 1983, PP. 19f

personnel, under the master's authority. Thus the sixteenth century definition of economics as 'discipline concerned with the correct management of house and family' is relevant to the situation in the parables.

The oikos of the parables alludes to the promised land and the chosen people, and remotely to the world in general and its inhabitants, over whom God is the Lord. In the Septuagint, oikoumene and katoikountes is translated 'world' and 'those who dwell therein' (Psalm 24:1). According to the rabbinic interpretation, "God is Lord of the house, for the whole world is his, and Moses is his oikonomos". Behind this interpretation stands Numbers 12:7 where the Lord speaks with Moses, who "is entrusted" with 'all my house'. From this, a direct line runs to the New Testament, Jesus is compared with Moses (Hebrews 3:1-6), and Jesus, therefore, has dominion, if we then take note of this, the relationship of Jesus' teaching to economics becomes clear.[19]

Biblical economics is closely connected with politics, as economics is simply seen as a function of the political structure. This is summed up in the pronouncement of Jesus, "Render to Caesar the things that are Caesar's and to God the things that are God's (Matthew 22:21). The New Testament knows nothing about economic order that is independent of the political order. The Bible in effect takes note of the fact that wealth is a very powerful force in human relationships with God. Nevertheless Christians keep away from preaching a

19. Arend Th, Van Leeuwen, "Toward an Economic Theology", Theology Digest, Vol. 22, No. 2, Summer 1974, Pp. 160-161

total economic well-being of man, and that is the essence of the Gospel. The Christian message has fallen short, then the word of the world market has taken over.

Christian's message must agree with economics' on a platform where both sides can ask sensible questions and give intelligible solution to them. Theology and economics must work hand in hand. Thus Jesus never shunned economic activities of his time but this must be in line with the principles of the kingdom he came to establish.

3.2 WEALTH AND POVERTY IN RELATION TO THE KINGDOM OF GOD:

Let us begin here by taking note that to Jesus, to get the kingdom of God is more than any material possession and that ought to be so, since, "the earth is the Lord's and the fullness therefore, the people and those who dwell therein" (Psalm 24:1). Hence, Jesus taught that the wise choice for one to make (since all is God's), to be rich in the true sense of it, would be to "seek first the kingdom of God and its righteousness and the other things shall then automatically belong to him. (Matthew 6:33).

Those who belong to God are indeed rich but he took time to warn that "a man's life does not consist in the abundance of his possessions" (Luke 12:15b). He then warned on the danger of covetousness in which he gives the rich fool as an epitome.

Covetousness appears about nineteen times in the New Testament. It occurs oftener in the Authorized Version than it does in the Revised Standard Version. The word translated covetousness in the A.V. is the Hebrew word betas, which basically means dishonest gain. In Greek, the word is pleonexia which means striving for material possession[20]. This is a word that has its origin from the Ten Commandment. It was a breach of this commandment which brought disaster to the Israelites camp after their capture of Jericho usually known as the sin of Achan. It is regarded as a terrible sin, and sternly condemned.

To the Greek and the Roman this word pleonexia described a detested quality. It comes from two Greek words which always wants more, and wants it in the ugliest way. It is used to describe over-reaching ambition, shameless cupidity, and conscienceless rapacity. The Roman's described it in two vivid phrases. They called it amor sceleralus habendi, the accursed love of having, and they called it iniurisoa appetitio alienorum, the beneful desire for that which belongs to others. It is a hungry desire for that which a man has no right to have[21].

Covetousness could be a root from which other sins spring. It could be regarded as greed and that was what Jesus warns about. Covetousness could be in form of struggle for prominence or position; like the case of the Pharisees (Matthew 23:5-7), the two sons of Zebedee – James and John

67

20. Ronald J. Sider, Rich Christians in the Age of Hungere, Paulist Press, New York, 1977, P. 122.
21. William Barclay, The Plain Man's Guide to Ethics, Fount Paper Back, Glasgow, 1984, P. 196f

(Mark 10:35-45), and the disciples' argument in who is the greatest among them (Luke 22:24-27). This kind of covetousness can beget envy and jealousy. Envy is manifested in a variety of ways and could lead to murder and other vices. Covetousness is a sin which Jesus does not want his disciples to get into in any form, because it could block one's way to the kingdom and remarked after the parable of the rich fool, "So is he who lays up treasure for himself, and is not rich toward God". Therefore to be truly rich means investment into the kingdom and its mission.

True riches in Jesus teaching are that in recognition that they belong to God, who is ruler over man's life. The realization of this made Jesus to call his disciples to a joyful life of carefree concern for possession (Luke 12:22-30). He wants them to know that riches alone could not provide the good life but the kingdom matters, and those who are concerned more about money and property are not children of the kingdom. He therefore, advises, "Seek his kingdom, and these things shall be yours as well (Luke 12:31). A place in the kingdom of God is true riches.

It is this kingdom of God that Jesus came proclaiming. Mark tells us that Jesus began his preaching in Galilee with the message, "The time is fulfilled, and the kingdom of God is at hand" (Mark 1:15). What Jesus came to proclaim was a new community – The Israel of God that will embrace people of all races at heavenly banquet[22].

22.   R.T. France, Jesus The Radical, IVP, England, 1989. P. 143.

God's kingdom is wherever God is in control, his sovereignty is accepted and his will is obeyed. When one submits to God's claim on him, there in essence the kingdom of God has already come – using Jesus' own language, he has entered the kingdom of God. There is still a sense in which the kingdom is still being expected, when everyone comes to recognize the sovereignty of God and in that sense we can pray, "Your Kingdom come", until God's will is done on earth as it is in heaven, when Jesus himself returns in glory, the Son of Man to whom "was given authority, honour and royal power, and his Kingdom would never end. (Daniel 7:14).

However, we can still say in a sense, "Yours is the Kingdom". Much of what Jesus said about the Kingdom of God relate not to that ultimate consummation, but to God's kingship as it was already being seen, as the powers of evil fled in disarray, and men and women found themselves through the ministry of Jesus into a right relationship with God. That was the kingdom Jesus came to establish, a kingdom 'not of this world" (John 18:33-37), but with an effect on life in this world which will have no rivalry and which will only be fully established when everyone everywhere gladly acknowledges the sovereignty of God[23].

Let us now examine what Jesus teaches in relation to the kingdom and these possessions.

23. Ibid, P. 147

(A) THE KINGDOM AND MONEY

The pursuit of wealth is diametrically opposed to the pursuit of God or the kingdom of God[24]. They are two things that cannot go together: that is mammon and God are like two masters. Professor S.O. Abogunrin quoting J.S. Ana writes concerning mammon, "It promises wealth, but creates poverty; it speaks of liberty, but enslaves, and demands allegiance of the hearts of mankind". Jesus says: Mammon and God cannot be served together"[25]

Mammon according to the New World Dictionary Concordance to the New American Bible, is an Aramaic word used in some translations, meaning property, wealth. It is read in some statements of Jesus, with negative connotations, to condemn the almost idolatrous attachment to riches which is incompatible with the honour due to God (Matthew 6:24, Luke 16:13). He calls it the "Mammon of iniquity", or filthy lucre, to condemn the injustice that too often accompanies riches (Luke 16:9-11).

To John L. McKenzie, S.J. mammon[26] is personified in opposition to God, and it is found in the Talmud to designate not only money, but possessions in general. When we examine it together with Matthew 6:19-21 and the following passage, the radical character of the teaching of Jesus on wealth and ownership begins to emerge. Material possessions are a false god that demands exclusive loyalty as God demands it. The claims of material possession must be totally repudiated.

70

24. Ibid, P. 147
25. A.W. Tozer, The Pursuit of God, Scripture Union (Nig) Press and Book Limited, Ibadan, 1987, pp. 21-30.
26. John L. McKenzie, Comment on Mattew. The Jerome Biblical Commentary (ed. Raymond Brown, et al. Geoffrey Chapman, London, Vol. II, 1980, P. 74.

To Jesus, no compromise is possible with mammon and the kingdom. Jesus' saying about money and possessions are frequently regarded as amongst the 'hardest' in the gospels. Most Christians tend to water them down. The most astounding statement about the Kingdom of God is not that it was near, but it would be the Kingdom of the poor and that the rich, as long as they remain rich, would have no part in it (Luke 6:20-26).

In explaining this passage of Luke 6:20ff. William Barclay says that if you set your heart and bend your whole energies to obtain the things which the world values, you will get them – but that is all you will ever get. In the expressive modern phrase, literally, you have had it. However, if on the other hand you set your heart and bend all your energies to be utterly loyal to God and true to Christ, you will run into all kinds of trouble; you may by the world's standard look unhappy, but much of your payment is still to come, and it will be joy eternal[27].

It is as impossible for a rich man to enter the kingdom as it would be for a Camel to be threaded through the eye of a needle (Mark 10:24-27). The Greek word for a Camel is kamelos. In this age of Greek there was a tendency for the vowel sounds to become very like each other, and there was word which would sound almost exactly the same – the word kamilos, which means a ship's hawser. It may well be that what Jesus said was that it would be easier to thread a needle

71

27. William Barclay, The Gospel of Luke, The Westminster Press, Philadephia, 1975, P. 76.

with a ship's hawser than for a rich man to enter the kingdom of God[28].

What the above portray is that it would take a miracle to get a rich man into the kingdom of God and that would not be to get him to give up all his wealth so that he could enter a kingdom of the poor. What the rich man in the gospel story was asked to do was to free himself from being enslaved by his possessions. In explaining this issue William Barclay quoted an apocryphal gospel of Hebrew which has some remains and it reads, "The other rich man said to Jesus, "Master, what good thing must I do really to live?" Jesus said to him, "Man, obey the Law and the Prophets'. He said, 'I have done so", Jesus said to him, "Go, sell all that you possess, distribute it among the poor, and come, follow me'. The rich man began to scratch his head, because he did not like this command. The Lord said, to him, "Why do you say that you have obeyed the Law and the Prophets" For it is written in the Law, "You must love your neighbour as yourself" and look you – there are many brothers of yours, sons of Abraham, who are dying of hunger, and your house is full of many good things and not one single thing goes out of it to them, and he turned and said to Simon, his disciple, who was sitting beside him, 'Simon, son of Jonas, it is easier for a camel to go through the eye of a needle than for a rich man to enter the Kingdom of Heaven[29].

Jesus' saying concerning the rich was to his disciples a hard saying hence they became astonished and asked, "Then

72

28. Ibid. P. 229
29. Ibid. P. 229

who can be saved". This shows that they did not even see themselves as poor in the material things. Therefore, if it is tough like this for a rich man to enter, then they too would have no place. However what Jesus was trying to teach is a right attitude to possession. If a man's god is that to which he gives all his time, his thought, his energy, his devotion, then wealth was his god. If he was ever to find happiness he must do away with all that and live for others with the same intensity as that with which he had so long lived for himself.

In the kingdom of God there is no place for the rich and no reward, and no consolation for them there. This could be what the rich man in the parable in Luke 16:19-31 wanted to warn his brother about. It follows that setting one's heart on the kingdom of God and subscribing to its values entails selling all one's possessions and making one's treasure in heaven which is true riches.

The ancient Palestinian Peasant or Labourer had very little opportunity to use hard money, and when it came into his hands his instinct was to bury it rather than spend it. He was especially moved to hide his little store of coins at times of political disturbance and there was always the danger of thieves or robbers. The saying tells the disciple that no lasting treasure can be stored on earth[30].

In Palestine, wealth was often made up of costly raiment; the moths could get at the fine clothes and eat them up but if a man's soul is clothed with the garments of honour,

73

30. John L. McKenzie, Op.city P. 74

purity and goodness, nothing can destroy it. If a man sets his heart to seek the treasures of heaven, that heart will be fixed on heaven, but if he seeks the treasures of earth, then his heart will be hooked to earth – and some day he must say good-bye to them, as the grim Spanish proverb has it, "There are no pockets in a shroud[31]. (Cf Matthew 6:19-21, Luke 12: 33-34, 14:33). Jesus shows that one must count the cost of entering into that community that totally belongs to God.

(B)   THE KINGDOM AND PRESTIGE

In the society in which Jesus lived, the dominant value was prestige. Prestige in the oriental world is till today the most valuable asset of any man and people would rather commit suicide than lose it. The society of that time was structured that everyone had a place on the social ladder. Account must be taken of this social ladder in anything that has to be done or said. It was important to recognize status and people lived of the honour and respect which others gave them.

Prestige and status were based upon ancestry, wealth, authority, education and virtue. They were signified and maintained by the way you dressed and were addressed, by whom you entertained socially and who invited you to their table and by where you were placed at a banquet or where you sat in the synagogue. Status was just as much part of religion as it was part of social life. Even the most strict and

74

31. John L. McKenzie, Op.city P. 74

fanatical of pious Jews, people of the Qumran, relied on their status and rank within their religious community[32].

Jesus roundly contradicted all this. He saw it as one of the fundamental structures of evil in the world and he dared to hope for a kingdom in which class differences would be meaningless. Jesus criticized the Pharisees who sat in their synagogue facing the congregation. They were anxious to gain public admiration, but Jesus compared them with 'unmarked' or 'unwhitened graves'. Jesus mentioned four things these men liked which shows their quest for preference and recognition: to walk about in the long robes of the scholars, to receive salutations in public places, to sit in the chief synagogue seats (while the congregation stood), and to have the places of honour at feast. Their long prayers were but 'a cloak for greed' (John 5:44, 12:43), Matthew 23:7-8). Jesus was not being unjust to them as Talmud refers to some of the Pharisees as a 'plague'[33].

Anyone who is concerned about prestige would have no portion in the kingdom. Hence Jesus used the child as a symbol of lowliness demanded of one who would enter the kingdom, when the disciples asked about who would be the greatest in the kingdom. Putting a child in their midst he said, "Truly, I say to you, unless you turn and become like children you will <u>never</u> enter the kingdom. (Matthew 18:3). True riches therefore, means the position of nothingness in recognition of the sovereignty of God.

75

32. Albert Ndan, <u>Jesus before Christianity</u>, Orbis Books Mary Knoll, New York, 1976, p. 54.
33. A. Elwood Sanner, <u>Beason Bible Commentary: The Gospel</u> of Mark, Beacon Hill Press Missouri, 1979, P. 378.

3.3 WHO ARE THE POOR IN JESUS TEACHING

The 'poor' are those who realize their own abject helplessness and the wealth of the riches of the grace of God. They are the people that Jesus regarded as poor, that is, any man who realized that things mean nothing, and God means everything[34].

Poverty to Jesus does not mean asceticism. Jesus and his disciplines are not depicted in the Gospel as adopting voluntary poverty or living a secluded life. John says that the twelve had a common fund and common cash-box kept by Judas Iscariot (John12:6, 13:29), but having all or some things in common is not the same as practicing poverty[35] or asceticism. Let us briefly see what asceticism means.

Asceticism is what some may regard as holy poverty. It is that branch of theological life which is concerned with man's way to perfection, and ultimately to union with God. It is calculated to produce saints, and is consequently practical as well as speculative. It sees the spiritual life as a fight to be won when man co-operates with God – and as a ladder to be climbed. Everything here is mapped out very meticulously, and no aid to the Christian's inner life is neglected, no danger left without its signpost. This is a life, whereby active charity to one's neighbour serves as an exercise in self-renunciation and as an attack on the passions[36]. In the Roman Catholic setting asceticism is an instrument in the pursuit of holiness.

76

34. William Barclay, <u>The Gospel of Matthew</u>, The Westminster Press, Philadelphia, 1975, Vol. 1, P. 92.
35. J.A. Ziesler, <u>Christian Asceticism</u>, S.P.C.K., London, 1973, P. 45.
36. Ibid, P. 6-7

This ascetic idea gave rise to a movement of poverty from the 11th century, which was the desire to conform this life to the gospel of Christ. In this we have men like Peter Damian, the Pataria in Milan. There was the struggle by the Gregorians to rid the spiritual life of its bondage to the goods of this world and its call to witness the very sources of the spiritual life, to forge links with the communal poverty of the primitive church of Jerusalem. They chose a lifestyle of humiliation purposely[37] in order to be spiritual.

We have others who took to voluntary poverty like St Bonaventure[38], the Roman Catholic Monks and nuns; St Francis of Assissi, etc. For St Thomas Aquinas, voluntary poverty was in no sense perfection itself, but only a means to perfection. To him the idea was the common possession of a moderate amount of goods, according to the specific purpose of each institution, these goods being acquired and managed in a peaceful way and in due time, so as to reduce pre-occupation with them to minimum.

Jesus never taught anything of the ascetic notion that forsaking food, possessions or sex is inherently virtuous. To be sure "these goods are", as St. Augustine puts it, "only rings from our beloved, they are not the beloved himself. They are part of God's creation and sign of his love. If we treasure them as good tokens of his affection instead of mistaking them as the beloved, they are marvelous gifts which enrich our lives[39].

37. Luke T. Johnson, Sharing Possessions: Mandate and Symbol of Faith, Fortress Press, Philadelphia, 1981.
38. Wayne, Hellmann, "Poverty". The Franciscan way to God" Theology Digest, Vol. 22, No. 4, Winter, 1974, P. 339.

Jesus himself was never ascetic. He joined in the marriage celebration in which his first miracle was said to have taken place (John 2:1-11). He dined with the prosperous as well as the outcast. In his own words he said, "The son of Man came eating and drinking, and they say, "Behold, a glutton and a drunkard, a friend of tax collections and sinners" (Matthew 11:19). There is no such thing in Jesus' teaching as virtue of poverty, but there are certainly virtuous demands concerning the possession and use of everything which one can hold claim to. There must be gathered up into the thrust of a consecration to living absolutely the love of God and one's neighbour[40] .

The gospels regard the poor as those who are marginalized on earth. They can be regarded as those who are truly Jesus disciples who left all and followed him. (Mark 1:18). There are the 'poor' court (Luke 6:20). These, Jesus said are blessed. They have no security, no possessions to call their own, not even a foot of earth to call their home, no earthly society to claim their absolute allegiance. For 'Jesus' sake they have lost all. Jesus said that to these belong the kingdom of God.

This may not mean stripping oneself every material possession. It could be living in such a spirit as could be read in first beatitude "Blessed are the poor in spirit" (Matthew 5:3). This could mean the disciples' spirit of renunciation. This kind of poor is called 'the Lord's poor, the poor of the flock,

78

40. Yves Congar, "Poverty in Christian life Amidst an Affluent Society", War, Poverty, Freedom: The Christian Response, Vol. 15 (ed.) Franze Bockle, Paulist press, N.Y. 1966, p.97.

the disciple-poor". They are blessed because their cry is to God-ward. These are the spiritual poor.

This is the type which Gongar and Metz view through the example of Jesus, as descent to the condition of the lowest, and taking uncomplainingly on oneself all the consequences of guilt of poverty and slavery, suffering and death by crucifixion, and even descent into hell, without any desire for revenge. It is a situation whereby one could give up anything or everything for the sake of his soul. It is self-denial. Jesus says, "For what shall it profit a man, if he gains the whole world and forfeits his life" or what shall a man give in return for his life. (Matthew 16:26). It is the awareness of one's finiteness, restriction and death[41]. Therefore these are the little band who for the sake of Christ renounced all. They have a hidden treasure that is stored through the way of the cross[42]. Then what does it cost to be a disciple?

3.4 THE COST OF DISCIPLESHIP

Discipleship was a common practice among Jewish rabbis at the time of Jesus. Those who wished to be disciples chose their masters, but in Jesus' own case it was not so. Jesus called his disciples and chose them (John 15:16). Those who volunteered to follow Jesus were confronted with the stark reality of following him. He said, "Foxes have holes, and birds of the air have nests, but the Son of man has nowhere to lay his head" (Luke 9:58). There were those who refused to follow

41. John Metcalfe, The Beatitudes: The Publishing truth, Buckinghanshire, London 1993, P.2. See also: James Mantgomey Boice, The Sermon on the Mount Ministry Resources Library, Grand Rapids, 1988, Pp. 21f.
42. Dietrich Bonhoeffer, The Cost of Discipleship, SMC Press Limited, London, 1959, P. 97

him as he called for the concern of the world and he remarked, "No one who puts his hands to the plough and looks back is fit for the kingdom of God (Luke 9:62). Jesus was calling anyone who would be a disciple to join in a mission which was always dangerous, and was eventually to lead them into serious trouble. He passed through trouble and disciples would not be greater than their masters.

Jesus called disciples from all sorts of endeavour. There were the rich and the poor and the outcast. For instance, the inner circle seem to have been from the 'middle class' background as Jesus. They were partners in a fishing business thriving enough to employ workers and Thomas and Nathaniel were in the same line of business. Matthew the tax collector would have needed a reasonable degree of education to have qualified him for his job. Luke recorded some women followers who were sufficiently wealthy to contribute to the group's support[43]. (Luke 8:3). One characteristic marks the response of these men and women to Jesus' call, "They left all and followed him". This formed Peter's comment to Jesus Lo; we have left everything and followed you".

What does it then cost to be a disciple of Jesus? To accept the call to discipleship was, in a sense to give up even one's life. (Mark 8:35). He emphasized the importance of the cross in discipleship, "if any man would come after me, let him deny himself and take up his cross and follow me' (Mark 8:34). This issue of the cross was hard for the disciples to

43. R.T. France, Op.cit, P. 64

accept, Peter, who had just made his great confession of faith, took Jesus aside. He felt that he should 'rebuke' his Master for thinking and speaking even of his own death. In Matthew 16:22, it is put thus: "God forbid, Lord! Yet Jesus 'rebuked Peter'. He was on the side of God. He was not thinking in human way that would always choose to avoid suffering. Peter was even 'satan' to him. Discipleship means death not only to self-centered living, but being willing for Christ's sake to suffer shame and pain at the hands of the world[44]. Discipleship was not for those who cared too much what others thought of them.

To be a disciple would be not living according to the dominant characteristics of human society as it is known. They are ideals that would look stupid to the secular people. It is a life of humility. Following Jesus is meant to be a flattering occupation[45]. They must avoid ostentation, caring only for what God thought of them (Matthew 6:1-18).

From the above we could realize that following Jesus means a radical nothingness. The demand of Jesus is quite contrary to our natural self-centeredness and no wonder why this proved too much for the disciples. Some find it difficult to join like the rich young man whom Jesus told frankly to do away with all that he possesses. Others who joined earlier went away as Jesus' real intentions became very clear. Even Peter the pillar of the disciples denied ever knowing Jesus when the going got tougher and he could not face the

44. Francis Foulkes, How the Goodnews began: Study Guide to Mark's Gospel, African C.P. Ghana, 1986, P.136.
45. R.T. France, Op. cit, P. 72 CF. Fulton J. Sheen, Life of Christ, Pan Book Limited, London, 1958, P. 175

challenge. It is costly to be Jesus disciple because he came to serve and not be served and give his life as ransom. His disciples must join in his mission. He warned the would-be disciples of the need of counting the cost in two parables in Luke 14:28-33 and concluded: "Therefore, whoever of you does not renounce all that he has cannot be my disciples".

3.5   JESUS' CONCERN FOR THE POOR

At the time of Jesus what was probably the most serious social division, as it is now, was the gap between the rich and the poor. What then was Jesus' attitude to this situation? Jesus' concern for the poor could be said to be that of total identification. Let us trace this from his background. He is the Immanuel, who took up lowly place and way of birth.

If we consider Nathaniel's remark in John 1:46, "Can anything good come out of Nazarath? We will note that location is more than a matter of geography. Nathaniel's question places Jesus in a background part of an underdeveloped area with a bad reputation. The question is quite dismissing and contemptuous. Jesus belonged to the despised people and was willing to admit it. His location tells who he was.

Jesus' ministry was from Nazareth in Galilee and finally terminated in Judea, back in Jerusalem. This showed to whom he belonged and with whom he wanted to be identified: the despised, those to whom full human existence was denied. The name he preferred "the Son of Man", has as its deepest meaning identification with the least among people and as it was in life, so in death: the way led to the cross and complete identification with the rejected, a thief and a murderer. Even at this his death, the location was significant, he died 'outside the gate'... (Hebrews 13:13). Even at his resurrection, he went back first to Galilee where he started, back among his own – the poor. Galilee, with its poor and its insurgents, the land where the eschaton was itching to come to life, became the explosive basis of the gospel of the kingdom[46].

Jesus was neither ashamed of his background from the despised village of Nazareth, nor of being the son of a carpenter. The gospel writers did not try to 'upgrade' him socially. Like most of the others in the Nazareth village, Jesus would have experienced periods of poverty and times of hunger. He lived in an environment where poverty is known. He himself was no poor beggar, but he was indeed one of the people on the margins. He lived and moved among them and took their side. He carried out his ministry in a typical rural environment and quite understood their problems.

Therefore, like the prophets before him, he spoke from a position of close observation of the realities of the situation around him. He would have seen the hard slog of life on the farms and in the vineyards. He would have heard the complaints of those burdened by heavy debts, the murmurs against absentee landlords by aggrieved tenants, the gambling

83

46. Coeraad Boenad, The Poor side of Europe, WCC Publication, Geneva, P. 48.

against tax-collectors. He would have felt the mood of fathers whose sons opted out of the slog and ran into search of their imagined good life, or whose daughters went into prostitution to pay debts that never seemed to reduce. He would have noticed violent occasions on the roads, fatal accidents on building projects, crucified criminals[47].

So in launching out into his ministry on a Sabbath day in the synagogue he opened and read from Isaiah 61, and proclaimed that "this scripture was being fulfilled..." that is, that his mission was to be among the poor and for their sake the portion reads: "The Spirit of the Lord is upon me, because he has anointed me to preach good news to the poor. He has sent me to proclaim release to the captives...to proclaim the acceptable year of the Lord" (Luke 18-19).

This last phrase in the above passage could have been drawn from the idea of the year of Jubilee as in Leviticus 25. (This year of Jubilee we have explained in chapter two of this book). Some scholars have suggested that Jesus came here calling for the real year of Jubilee to be in practice, that is, a radical programme of debt cancellation and redistribution of land. At that period under Rome that would mean a revolution. Some scholars have also suggested that Jesus did not call for a literal operation of the Levitical law, but rather quoted from the prophetic use of jubilary ideas as a way of characterizing his minsitry[48]. Nevertheless, one thing is sure,

47. Chris Wright, <u>Knowing Jesus through the Old Testament</u> Marshal, London, 1992, P. 227.
48. Ibid, P. 228

with this inaugural reading, Jesus had declared his mission as for the poor.

To Jesus it pleases God to give to the poor his kingdom and that he came to proclaim. The special feature of this kingdom was a programme of good news, the poor. Jesus put this in practice through a revolution in the meaning of service. What is Jesus attitude to wealth and poverty is a balance economic adjustment. Taking its root from the Old Testament Jubilee principles. J. Sider wondered how it would be if Christians could observe one year as a year of Jubilee, when every debt would be cancelled, every land and other things returned to the original owners. That may mean there would be no poor Christian[49] but even the tithe issue, are Christians who preach it practicing it to the letter? They only collect for the store house (the church), even from the poor without responding to their needs.

There is need for Christians to apply what J. Sider calls Economic koinonia[50]. Koinonia in classical Greek means association or a partnership. In later Greek koinonain is used as the opposite and contracts of pleonexia, which is the grasping spirit out for itself. Thus koinonia is the spirit of generous sharing as contrasted with the spirit of selfish getting. In secular Greek koinoni is used to express a close and intimate relationship into which people enter[51].

In the Christian life, a koinonia means 'practical sharing' with those less fortunate. Paul uses the word three

85

49.   Ronald Sider, op.cit, p. 92
50.   Ibid., P. 103
51.   William Barclay, New Testament Words, S.C.M. Press Limited, London, 1976, P. 173

times in connection with the collection he took from his churches for the poor saints at Jerusalem (Romans 15:26, II Corinthians 8:4,9:13, cf Hebrews 13:6). The Christian koinonia is that bond which binds Christians to each other, to Christ and to God. The present economic relationships in the world wide body of Christ are really unbiblical, sinful, hindrance to the Gospel of Christ and a desecration of the body and blood of Jesus Christ[52].

It is sinful for small number of people in the world to be living in affluence while many suffer without their concern. We see so many people who suffer for lack of minimal health care, education, even enough food to eat. The present class structure in the church and the place the rich occupy without stewardship is a hindrance to the gospel.

The kingdom of God is not anti-material or even anti-riches but God's purpose as expressed through Jesus is that all share in the riches, and the call of Jesus is that those who are now rich should give to others. Most of his parables are about bridging divisions of wealth and property through generosity.

52. R.J. Sider, op.cit., P. 110

4

THE GOSPEL OF PROSPERITY

AND THE GOOD NEWS TO

THE POOR

In this chapter we shall try to examine what is meant by the Gospel, its different ideas. We shall trace the origin of the preaching on prosperity and then try to know how it is being preached today. Then we shall see if the gospel has any message to the poor.

4.1   THE GOSPEL DEFINED

The word "Gospel" or "Good News" has its source from the Greek word <u>euaggelion</u>. This word is so specifically and characteristically a Christian word that it has not a long history outside the New Testament. It is in New Testament that euaggelion becomes a tremendous word. It is the word used in summarizing the whole Christian message (Mark 1:1, 1 Corinthians 15:1). The kingdom preached by Jesus is 'good news' (Matthew 4:23, 9:33, and 24:14). The word euaggelion appears seventy-two times in the New Testament signifying its centrality to the Christian message. Out of this 72 times, 54 of it are in Paul's letters. There is a contrast. The preaching of John the Baptist with its consuming fire, its winnowing fan, its axe laid to the root of the tree is the reverse of good news. It is tidings of disaster, but the whole essence of the message of Jesus is 'good news of God'.

The euaggelion is atimes spoken of as the euaggelion 'of God' (Mark 1:14; 1 Thessalonians 2:2, 8, 9). In two senses it means the good news of God.

(a)   It showed men a God whose heart was love.

(b)   It is 'sent by God'. It was through the initiative of God that salvation came to man. "For God so loved the world that he sent his only begotten son" (John 3:16).

(c)   Sometimes, it is spoken of as the euaggelion of "Jesus Christ" (Mark 1:1, 1 Cor. 4:4). This is so because Jesus 'brought' it to men, and he was its embodiment. He did not only tell men what God was like, he showed them the Father. Sometimes Paul uses expression "My" or "Our" eugggelion showing that a man must pass it through his mind and receive it unto his heart until it is utterly and inalienably his.

(d)   The euaggelion is for all men (Mark 13:10, 16:15, Acts 15:7).[1]

There are other things about the euaggelion. It is a revelation from God that must be believed in, which is entrusted to Man to proclaim. It is also something for which one could 'risk everything', in its service and defence. It can be hindered, refused and twisted or distorted. Furthermore, euaggelion is the good news of truth, hope, peace; it is also of the promises of God, it is immortal, it is of the risen Christ and salvation of mankind.

Having explained what the gospel means, let us now try to branch into different kinds of gospels as is being conceived today.

(1)   The Social Gospel

This is a term associated with the rise of modernism and liberalism, so we also have liberal social gospel[2]. The emphasis is upon the Church becoming significantly involved in the social and political life of the contemporary society. According to the liberal, the 'de'socialization' of Christianity has led to the Church's one-sided preaching of salvation of the soul for the hereafter, while it has neglected to meet the social and economic needs of the world, and help in relieving the world sufferings here and now. To the social gospels,

1.   William Barclay, New Testament Words, S.C.M. Press Limited, London, 1976, pp.101-2.
2.   Carl F.H. Henry, Christian Personal Ethics, Baker Book House, Grand Rapids, Michigan, 1979, P. 282

Christians should work for reforms in the political and economic spheres. A Christian should strive for such things as world peace, prison reforms, racial equality, human rights, and tolerance among the differing political ideologies and religions of the world. They frequently appeal to what they call "the social concern of the prophets in Israel", and to "the ethical principles of the teachings of Jesus in an effort to find scriptural support to their "Christian socialism" (or social Gospel)[3].

(2)   Modernism is another type

It refers to anything that is up-to-date, current, or new. Religious modernism began with the rise of the new liberal trends in theology – modern-day agnosticism, anti-supernaturalism, the rejection of the inerrancy of scripture, and the unscriptural reinterpretation of the Christian faith[4].

(3)   The Liberation Gospel

This is what gave rise to what is known today as the liberation theology. This theology arises out of a concern to interpret the gospel in the context of the sufferings of the poor, and their cry for justice and freedom, their cry for humanity and dignity. The task of the theologian is not only to listen to the word of God, but to listen to the cry of the poor, the powerless and oppressed and interpret the word in that context[5]. Rebecca Chopp defines it thus as quoted by Torrance.

90

3.   Hobert E. Freeman, Every Wind of Doctrine, Reprinted Faith Builder Publication, Aba Nig. 1987, pp. 101-105.
4.   Ibid, Pp. 94-95.
5.   Alan J. Torrance, "The Theology of Liberation in latin America", Different Gospels (ed.) Andrew Walker, Hodder and Stoughton, London, 1988, P. 183.

"To understand liberation theology, we must grasp one basic claim: suffering and its quest for freedom is the fundamental reality of human experience as well as the location of God, Christ and the Church in history. Liberation theology urges action, strategy, and change in human existence; it demands justice, equality, and freedom in Christian witness. Consequently, liberation theology is a new language of God, seeking, in the present historical situation, to be the voice of those who suffer[6].

The primary concern of liberation theology is the proclamation of the gospel. Theology is not undertaken in order to write books, but to contemplate the church's mission and aid gospel proclamation. Proclaiming God's Kingdom means proclaiming the kingdom of life, the fullness of life, whether individual, social, spiritual or material[7]. This theology wants to find answers to how the Gospel could be proclaimed in a suffering world.

Let us now move on to an important aspect of the gospel which is now known as the Prosperity Gospel. This is part of the focus of this chapter.

4.2   THE ORIGIN OF THE GOSPEL OF PROSPERITY

This is a sort of message which tends to lay much emphasis on wealth. To this sort of preaching, man's true relationship with God is tended to be measured by his material blessings. Gospel of Prosperity sees poverty and suffering as a

91

6.   Ibid., P. 184
7.   Gustavo Gutierrez, "Liberation Theology", Theology Digest, Vol. 35, No. 1, Springs, 1988, P. 32

curse, as a result of one's sins. It is the will of God for man to prosper and therefore, anyone who does not would have been estranged from God and should reconcile in order that he may prosper. This type of Gospel makes its appeal mostly to the Old Testament where every material possession is seen as a blessing from God and poverty a curse. References are made often to Abraham and Solomon. There is a general tendency within this circle to teach that every Christian must be on top saying, "You shall be head and not tail" (Deuteronomy 28:13). Before we go on, let me ask, if everyone becomes the head, who shall be the tail? Or is tail not important as the head? This gospel does not teach the spirit of contentment.

Let us try to trace briefly the origin of this type of Gospel. For it has been long in the history of Christianity. It began during the time of John Calvin after the peasant war of 1524. Calvin started with the crusade that religious matters were not more important than the worldly matters. Both spheres owe allegiance to the same Christ.

A Calvinistic Puritan was reported to have said a century later in the British Parliament: "Reformation must be universal, reform all places, all persons and callings, reform the benches of judgments, the inferior magistrate…reform the universities, reform the cities, reform the countries, reform inferior schools of learning, reform the Sabbath, reform the ordinances, the worship of God. Every plant which my heavenly Father has not planted shall be rooted up". It is also noted that at the same period an English writer said, "I had rather see coming towards me a whole regiment with swords, than one lone Calvinist convinced that he is doing the will of God"[8]

As soon as reformation came into Geneva, begging was outlawed. There was war on poverty and charity was not present. No beggars walked the streets of Geneva nor were there alms collections for the poor, because "abundant help is provided in a truly fraternal spirit". The poor do not exist according to Calvin in a sermon on Deuteronomy 15:11. They are your poor, your brother, your poor, your needy, says the Hebrew text. It is not that the rich give to the poor and the poor receive from the rich, but the rich should give to God and the poor should receive from God, "so that both praise the Lord". One of Calvin's supporters argued against private giving of alms. This was the job of the church in order to prevent arrogance in the giver.

Calvin connected justification with law. Whether one is a tailor, a merchant or a peasant, a Christian ought "in obedience and gratitude, to work for the renewal of the earthly community. Calvin did not hesitate to compare the Geneva grain merchants with "murderers", savage beasts, biting and eating up the poor, sucking in their blood'. This is because of their hoarding, in order to increase prices. To Calvin, the poor represent Jesus himself. Prosperity, then, is not something neutral, it is an instrument working for good or

8. Coenraad Boerma, The Poor Side of Europe, Risk Books Series, World Council of Churches, Geneva, 1989, P. 25

evil. Wealth is justified only if it is put to the service of those who are not wealthy.

The republic of Geneva at the time of Calvin was surrounded on all sides by enemies, and there were countless refugees. Geneva was also the birth place of spirit of resistance. It then began to develop into an important economic and political Centre. The privileged lived in luxury, while poverty increased among the under-privileged. Over against this development, Calvin called for solidarity, based on an understanding of the unity of spirit and matter.

Calvin only was concerned with the distribution of earthly goods, including the product of one's own labour. To him all people are equal before God. For Calvin, this democratic attitude was not only a political task, but also an economic calling. The State's role is to protect the poor from the rich and to achieve a harmony of interest. Calvin did not see private ownership as unlawful. For him, property was only unlawful when not used in a just and charitable way. In this case he remained mediaval[9].

We could see from the above that Calvin was more of a liberationist who realized the bad effect of poverty and would wish that it is abolished from the society completely. Calvin it is true, believed in the spirit of capitalism, but he had the passion for the poor that the rich Christians must know their responsibilities of harmonizing their possessions with those who have not. He sought for justice, equity and fair play. So

9. Ibid, p. 27.

there is a mark of difference between the gospels of prosperity as it was being preached in the past and now. We will examine how this is being preached now.

4.3 THE RECENT EMPHASIS ON PROSPERITY

What is it that is being peddled in so many Christian messages today, if not prosperity? Today the desire to acquire has replaced the passion for souls to be saved. Let us say quickly that the way and manner prosperity is being preached today posit danger rather than help to the church. As it is, so many preachers today are so earthly-minded and are of no heavenly use[10]. No one can deny that in the modern church set-up the main cause of anxiety is money. As what occupies most minds is how to get the resources. This is the hour when the average church knows more about promotion than prayer, has forgotten consecration by fostering competition – the winning church, the shining church, the conquering church, etc – and when the church has substituted propaganda for propagation, the age of prosperity gospel. Many preachers these days are fond of traveling than travailing, hence no births. This is a time when preachers mistake commotion for creation, action for unction and rattle for revival[11]. What do you see today? It is struggle for membership from one church to another. Buses – some even trailers are used in carrying members to our churches. However, is it really for passion about these souls or to make sure that the church is filled up?

95

10. Leonard Ravenhill, <u>Why Revival Tarries,</u> Send the Light Trust, London, 1972, P. 6
11. Ibid., P. 11

Today in Nigeria we have millions of churches (I guess), millions of bibles of different versions, endless preachers, still we are where we are-sinful. Preachers scramble for members and get them, but are they truly committed people? When a rich man enters any church today, it means catching a 'big fish', but when a poor man enters, he has brought problem for the church. Each church seeks to be more popular than the other, but it has not been in times of popularity that the true Church has always triumphed rather in adversity. The whole blame for the present international degeneration and corruption lies at the door of the Church. The Christian message today is substandard to the New Testament teaching especially on possession.

L. Ravenhill says that revival tarries today "because evangelism is so highly commercialized". He said, "The tithes of widows and of the poor are spent in luxury – living by many evangelists. The great crowds, great lines of seekers, great appreciation by the mayor, etc, are shouted to high heaven. All get publicity except the love offering" The poor dupes who give "think they do God service", while all they are doing is keeping a big reputation, small-hearted preacher living in Hollywood style"[12].

This is the reality of the church today. Today preachers are not for simple life-style. Most of them who have fleet of vehicles, estates, big bank balance, still beg for more. There are a lot of extortionist and unjust preachers today. Some who

96

12. Ibid, P. 13

never made it in other endeavours, who are not even qualified in any measure no longer change their suits once a day, but two or three times a day. They preach the Jesus of the stable, but themselves live in swank hotels. As Ravenhill puts it, "For their own lusts they bleed the audience financially in the name of the one who had to borrow a penny to illustrate this sermon. They wear expensive Hollywood suits (the best brocade "Agbada') in honour of one who wore a peasant's robe. They feast on three-dollar steaks in remembrance of the one who feasted alone in the desert. Today an evangelist is not only worthy of his hire (so he thinks), but of compound interest[13]. This is how degenerated Christian preaching has gone today. It is all prosperity not even of the soul, but of material. Let us, before we go further see some of the traits of many evangelists today.

(a)   Pride, or self-praise

According to an ancient adage, self-praise, "smells bad". In other words, it stinks up the works. C.R. Swindoll says that no matter how we prepare it, garnish it with little extras, stice and serve it up on our finest silver piece, the odor remains. No amount of seasoning can eliminate the offensive smell. Unlike a good wife, age only makes it worse. It is much like the poisoned rat in the wall – if it is not removed the stench becomes increasingly unbearable. Leave it untouched and within a span of time it will taint and defile everything

13. Ibid, P. 14.
14. Charles R. Swindoll, <u>Growing Strong in the Seasons of Life,</u> Multnomah Press, Oregon 1983, pp. 315-316

that comes near it[14]. Pride they say goes before a fall. "God resists the proud" says the Bible.

It is a common sight today to hear preachers who use the greater part of their preaching to brandish their positions only to say few things or nothing about Jesus Christ. You often times hear narratives of the places they have traveled to all over the world, the hotels they had slept in, the president or head of state of a country they have had hand-shake with, the miracles they have performed. The high places they have been to and how they have preached to kings and princes. We have indeed today, so many pompous preachers who see themselves so highly that they must be recognized with all their acquired titles of 'professors', 'doctor', 'most Revd', Most – senior/superior or apostle-founded-leader', etc. or else they would not stand up to preach. They must be introduced as renowned in the world preaching ministry and the audience must stand up for the preacher. Preachers today lack attitude of servants. It is very important to a preacher today, for everyone to know who he is, where he had been, how he had done, and what he wants. No spirit of humility. He brandishes his voice to show that he is American even when he has not been to Lagos.

Preachers want to receive honour from men – hypocrites. Jesus said of himself, "I do not receive glory from men"... and said of the hypocrites, "How can you believe, who receive glory that comes from one another and do not seek the glory that comes from the only God? (John 5:41, 44). Ravenhill said, "Away with all flashy backslapping and platform flattery! Away with this exalting of "My radio program", "my books! Oh, the sickening parade of flesh in our pulpits: "We are greatly privileged, etc." Speakers (who are there really by grace alone) accept all this, nay-even expect it! The fact is that when we have listened to most of those men, we would not have known they were great if they had not been announced so! We are filthy. We love men's praise. We "seek our own"[15].

Where are the unassuming and humble preachers like John the Baptist, like the apostle (Peter, Paul, etc?) like the early church fathers – Polycarp, Clement, Ignatius, etc[16]. Preachers like Martin Luther, John Calvin, John Wesley, St. Francis of Assisi, St John Chrystostom and others of blessed memory who through humility and sacrifice made the gospel message known to people of their ages. What about Samuel Ajayi Crowther and the early missionaries who were unassuming and humble?

The Bible never speaks well of pride and self-praise. It calls a proud heart "sin" (Proverbs 21:4). Jesus himself gave warnings concerning pride and self-praise. He said, "When you are invited by anyone to a marriage feast, do not sit down in a place of honour, lest a more eminent man than you be invited by him; and he who invited you will come and say to you, "Give place to this man", and then you will begin with shame

---

15. Leonard Ravenhill, op.cit, P. 15
16. See about those early Fathers through their writing: Early Christian Writings, Trans Maxwell Stamforth Pengiun Books, 1981.

to take the lowest place... for everyone who exalts himself will be humbled, and he who humbles himself will be exalted" (Luke 14:9, 11). He also said the same concerning the Pharisee and the Publican (Luke 18:9-14).

St Paul drives home this message in Galatians 6:3: For if anyone thinks he is something, when he is nothing, he deceives himself. There is no greater deception than self-deception. It is noticed almost in every preaching of today and the preachers. Atimes, we magnify our ability to do certain things and we also justify every action that we take. We often convince ourselves by self-deception that our actions are always right, when actually they are wrong. We do not see anything wrong in them, so long as it is done by us[17].

Having discussed pride and self-praise, let us now come to another trait of the recent gospel of prosperity, which Swindoll regards as monuments[18]. In this we see our churches and society saturated with these components – fortune, (materialism), fame, power, and pleasure.

Fortune is what our present age knows. It is boldly inscribed today in every aspect of the recent evangelical moves "Get rich". You always hear: "that preacher has made it!" if he is going on in Path-finder car or V-boot Mercedes Benz. In Nigeria where churches amass wealth and build mansions here, we have been led to believe that to know a true Christian church depends on how prosperous that church and her pastors are. Despite the fact that crime rates increase daily,

100

17. Honest U. Nwosu, Honesty as the way of Life, Emuje Printing, Akure, 1988, p. 30
18. Charles R. Swindoll, op.cit, p. 317

dishonesty and corruption everywhere noticed. The Church in Nigeria (even beyond) has been deceived into believing that the more right you are about what you believe, the more material blessings you have. But what can we do with the fact that Jesus had few material possessions to prove to the world that he was "blessed" by God?

To show off and prove that we are blessed, houses, temples, halls and whatever are built to the glory of God however to show that we created such a fortune, a large plaque is placed by the wall for everyone to see its reading: "Built for the glory of God by the Pride of Man". Thus all these desires for affluence have materialized.

Let us briefly assess materialism in the churches of today. Materialism has become the norm; people have grown to accept the suffocating materialism, consumptionism, and possessionism in the churches. Many Churches today spend millions of naira erecting places of worship and expanding the existing ones. Many have not invested in the ministry to the poor (this we shall come to). The New Churches (incorporated) would not establish in the rural areas where they feel they cannot make it materially. Most of these churches struggle to locate nearer to where the high-class people would attend and they do not mince words in telling you that this Church belongs to the rich.

Gregory Lewis sees the twentieth century Church which is ours, thus: "it is a Church with the mentality of the twentieth century, lost in its dilemmas, giving out hope with one breath, uttering signs of despair with the next. It is a Church that is locked into middle class existence, possess, consume, use up, get more, produce, do, act, cover up, act strong, don't give in, stand up for your rights, demand comfort, fight for convenience no matter how inconvenient the fight, press on, and if you have the money, buy it, if you have the pride, flaunt it, and if it feels comfortable, just hide in your programs... loving? Getting is loving. Possessing is loving, Consuming is loving and thus we are left right in the bosom of the enemy. We identify with the things of the world and our brand name "Christianity" does not have as its symbol the old rugged cross, but rather the new neon cross which lights up our Church for all to see"[19].

The Church today goes all the way to look for the money. God's grace in so many cases are for sale. An example of this could be seen in this report by Chioma Obi titled "Riddle of the Celestial Church Harvest Candle" she says, "For millionaires among celestial Church, harvest period is a period for acquiring more blessings and one way of doing it is buying the harvest water, honey and candle. There must be one candle for each parish at each harvest and the bargaining prices range between N50, 000 to N125, 000. Vintage people gathered that in 1987, the Transmission boss Monday Odiye bought the harvest candle of his parish for N70, 000; in 1988, for N95, 000. In the same parish in 1989, senior Evangelist

19. Gregory Lewis, Is God for sale?, Tyndale House Illionois, 1979, p. 43

Omotosho bought the candle at N125, 000. Thus, by 1990, it would cost N150, 000. They believe it could better their lives and boost their businesses thus they go to any extent to get the candle"[20].

Many criminals today are assured by prayer houses here and there that no matter their crimes, they could bring money and be prayed for against arrest. Many of these prayer houses are flourishing today in money given lavishly by drug barons.

Possessiveness is now in the vein of almost all churches in Nigeria. The Churches hold open the door to God's free grace with one hand, and with the other hand they may charge admission fee. Nothing in life is free, they would say. The Church has succumbed so much to our Nigerian mentality of measuring success by wealth. The total accumulated assets of religious property in Nigeria today could well be over N150 billion with all Churches taking in about N6 billion yearly – all tax free! How can a Church which claims to follow the Lord, having forsaken all, still heap up treasure for herself here on earth? Some are not even using it. The new evangelicals feel that this is a sign of God's blessing. This can be deduced from the preachings of these pastors on material prosperity.

Notable among these preaching in this way are: Archbishop – Professor Benson Idahosa of the Church of God Mission International Inc. who in Fame Magazine of 22nd and 28th February 1994 is regarded as an apostle of affluence and believes a man of God must live like a king. Pastor Enoch

20. Chioma Obi, Report – "Riddle of the Celestial Church Harvest Candle". Vintage People Ventage ventures Publication, Vol. 1 No. 34 March 30-April 5, 1990. P. 11

Adejare Adeboye of the Redeemed Christian Church of God Inc. These Ade Ojo regards as "mighty Apostles of the end-time Army of the Lord". These mighty men he said spare not those Christians who believe they are too conservative to believe and confess prosperity[21]. Another person is Olukolade the Pastor and District Suprintendent of the Church of God in Christ Pentecost Assembly Inc. Lagos who expresses his view on the prosperity of Christians in his book, "Your Power To Get Wealth". He sees Christians as being in a special covenant with God and therefore could not ever be poor. In expressing Christians as princess(es) of God and ambassadors – he concluded, "some too have got the power to get wealth"[22].

To Robert Tilton, it is unbelief that makes Christians un-wealthy. Every Christian has potential to create wealth so he says: "Now if you don't believe you are supposed to be prosperous or have the good things of this life, then you won't get very much. You have to desire to get out from under the influence of lack. God won't force you to take the good things which can be yours. As you think in your heart, so are you. So if you think lack, you will have lack". He asked, "Why settle for second Best?"[23]. Which means everybody must struggle for the best.

Some other preachers of this prosperity gospel preach that in order to be wealthy, it needs faithful payment of tithe forgetting that Jesus never commended the Pharisees who claim they pay their tithe, rather he commended the widow

21. Foluso Ade Ojo, Cripped by Greed, Gospel Publishers Lagos 1992, P. 15
22. Shola Olukolade, Your Power to get Wealth, Pentecostal Publishers, lagos 1992, P. 15.
23. Robert Tilton, Dare to be a success, Beulah Land Publishers, benin, 1987, P. 70.

who gave her mite – which was all she had. I would rather say here that material blessing is not the measure of relationship with God, as most of these are quite un-righteously acquired; especially in Nigeria where the processes of making money are unrighteous. There are so many poor people who are more blessed, some spiritually not materially – they have peace of mind, joy of their home, good health, etc. That may be hard for some of us to perceive since too many of us have long forgotten what it is to have spiritual wealth amidst poverty. The Churches today go all out for money and this has given birth to so many Churches.

Many reasons are attributive to the prosperity preachings of today and the materialism in the Church. The General Secretary of the Scripture Union of Nigeria attributed this to what he calls "privatization policy" that is now in the Church formation. Most of these Churches operate as ":sole proprietor type of business" having no constitution and the founders are not responsible to any other person and takes order from nobody and this gives room for self-aggrandizement.[24]

To Rt. Revd. G.O. Olajide, the Anglican bishop of Ibadan, Most of these new Churches are set up to maintain the founder and they seem to be materially rich because they have no missionary motive, hence they are mostly found in the townships and most of them may not survive persecution.[25]

24. Interviewed – bro Chris Okeke Scripture Union (Nig.) General Secretary 28/1/94.

25. Interviewed, The Rt. Rev'd G.O. Olajide, the Bishop of Ibadan, church of Nigeria (Anglican Communion), 28/1/94

Still on this gospel of prosperity there is an organization which could be said to be mostly for the rich. This is "The Full Gospel Businessmen Fellowship". This is the fellowship of the high class. According to Chris Okeke who relates with them, The Full Gospel Businessmen Fellowship is set up with a mission to reach the highly placed with the Gospel and this is done by using the means that would appeal to them. Hence the meetings are usually arranged at Hotels, banquet halls, etc. Okeke did not see this as preaching gospel of prosperity instead a way of bringing these class of the society to God. He advised that leaders of such group must also be ready to reach the poor – that is, becoming all things to all men[26].

Fame is another thing in this monument – "Be famous". People want popularity. There are no more preachers in John the Baptist form who will decrease and Jesus increases. Another thing is that so many people want to be in control. No one wants to be controlled. It was in the news for instance, concerning the breakage between Benson Idahosa of the Church of God and his erstwhile Pastor Ayo Oritesejafor of the Word of Life Bible Church, Warri, that they broke away as a result of power tussle and now Ayo is building one of the largest worship centers in Nigeria – Larger than that of Idahosa. To control.

Another thing is pleasure which Christians too feel that it is necessary to be enjoyed[28]. But every care must be taken in the seeking of pleasure to the neglect of Christian sacrifices.

26. Chris Okeke, op.cit.
28. William Bar lay, Ethics in a Permissive Society Founts Paperbacks, 1984, pp. 104-142

(Romans 12:1-2). People mistake pleasure for joy which is a fruit of the spirit.

Let us conclude this part of the chapter by quoting Thomas A. Kempis, "Those who perform great deeds have fallen to the depths, and have seen those who ate the food of angels enjoying the husk of pigs...how humble and meek I should feel when I look at myself! If I think I possess anything, how little I should value it! I must submit utterly to your fathomless judgments, I Lord, whose I find that I am nothing, but nothingness, utter nothingness. Immeasurable weight, impassable see, "There I can find nothing of myself but nothing."

Where can there lurk any trace of pride and confidence in my own goodness? All empty boasting is swallowed up in the depths of your judgments upon me. All mortal things are nothing in your sight – shall the clay bandy words with its fashioner?

How can a man whose heart is really subjected to God be moved to pride and empty boasting? The whole world will not move him to pride if the Truth really has his allegiance, and he will care nothing for all the praise of men if he has built his hopes upon God. For men are all nothing, and pass away like the sound of the words they speak, but the Lord remains faithful to his word for ever[29].

29. Thomas A. Kempis, The Imitation of Christ, Fount paperbacks Trans, Betty Knoth, 1984, Glasgow, pp. 131-132.

Having discussed the Gospel as well as the Gospel of prosperity (past and present), let us now try to see if the Gospel has any message for the poor.

4.4   THE MESSAGE FOR THE POOR

Jesus Christ demonstrated the same attitude toward the poor that God revealed in the Old Testament. Though the Saviour of all people, he looked with special compassion upon the poor. He purposely took the gospel to the poor, and specifically called attention to what he was doing[30]. He made the preaching of the gospel to the poor a validation of his own ministry. (Luke 4:18-21). He believed the poor were more ready and able to understand and accept his gospel (Matthew 11:25-28). He specifically directed the gospel call to the poor. He said, "Come to me, all who labour and are heavy laden, and I will give you rest" (Matthew 11:28). Jesus on several occasions recommended showing partiality to the poor (cf. Matthew 19:21, Luke 12:33, 14: 12-14).

Bringing good news is one of the different ways of describing liberation. It was part of Jesus liberating activity or praxis to evangelize or bring good news to the poor means to liberate them with the spoken word. Euaggelion (as we stated earlier) refers to the message which Jesus proclaimed to the poor and the oppressed. Good news for the poor means news that is hopeful and encouraging to the poor. Jesus brought the kingdom that belongs to the poor[31]. They are assured of a better future in the plans of God through the gospel. These are the poor spiritually who acknowledge their bankruptcy before God. They have no righteousness to offer, no merit to plead, no power to save themselves. They know that the only way to enter God's kingdom is to humble themselves like little children and receive it as a gift. To such, Jesus says: "Blessed are the poor in spirit, for theirs is the kingdom of Heaven". By contrast, the rich or self-satisfied, who imagine they have something to offer, are sent away empty.

In fact, the special concern in the gospel for the poor has led some authors like Bishop David Sheppard to feel that God is "bias to the poor". He stated, "I believe that there is a divine bias to the disadvantaged", and the Church needs to be much more faithful in reflecting it[32]. Therefore we could find out from the above that the gospel is meant originally for the poor spiritually and materially. (Luke 6:20-26).

We shall now proceed to the next chapter where we shall discuss implications of the above chapters to the Nigerian Christians – the Church.

32. David Sheppard, Bias to the Poor, Hodder and Stoughton 1983, p. 16.

5

IMPLICATIONS FOR THE

NIGERIAN CHRISTIANS

Before we treat this chapter let us look at how the situation is in Nigeria.

5.1   NIGERIAN SITUATION

There is already in Nigeria a serious problem of which her society is seriously struggling with. Full employment and good wages (which cannot even be guaranteed) will not yield the fruits expected of them if there is a scarcity of goods for ordinary consumers and if high productive and distributive costs put them beyond the reach of most Nigerians. Even so with the new burden of VAT upon the consumers. This is a predicament to which the country has found itself and this has been having serious psychological effects on the people. A solution is needed urgently to cushion this effect. Nigeria has passed from austerity measure to this present Structural Adjustment Programme. These measures have not helped matters in any because they are put in place to please the imperial nations and their institutions or agents IMF and others. What Nigeria needs now, according to the Archbishop of the Church of Nigeria (Anglican Communion), the Most Revd. J.A. Adetiloye is "Spiritual Adjustment programme". The unemployment rate, hunger crisis and moral decadence caught the Church with a common policy.

Nevertheless, a new visitor in Nigeria, seeing the rate with which Nigerians spend money buying expensive vehicles, live in expensive houses, both in and outside Nigeria, throw lavish parties, some in remembrance of someone who died 20 to 30 years back, and other expensive living would assume that all is well with Nigeria (in fact, so many clerics in the Church live 'high' and in affluence)[1], Ikoyi, Allen in Ikeja, and some parts of Lagos, it would seem as if there are no ghettos in Lagos. The way costly houses are springing up here and there daily it would seem that a bag of cement is below N100 and that there would soon be no people living under the bridge or in thatched houses. Still, any assessment of Nigeria as a rich nation would not be a mistake. Of course, Nigeria is a nation flowing with "milk and honey". Nigeria is rich in

1. Christian Treasury: An Independent Christian Magazine, December 1993, P. 1.

mineral resources and vast area of land for agriculture. She is an OPEC country[2], and therefore, supposed to be rich.

The problem is that the wealth of Nigeria is in the hands of few individuals while majority suffer in abject poverty. The nation itself is so debt-ridden that in its 1993 budget, it allocated N58.4 billion for debt servicing. This made some civil right activist to drag Shonekan's Transitional Council to court. They prayed the court to declare paragraphs 22.26 and 60 of Chief Shonekan's Budget speech as an indictment of President Babangida's misuse of public funds. African Concord quoted this paragraph 22 thus:

> *"The lack of fiscal discipline is the bane of our economy. In spite of realized revenue being above budgetary estimate, extra budgetary expenditure has been rising, so fast and resulting in even bigger deficit".*

Commenting on this, Dr. Ayo Akinbobola a political science teacher in University of Lagos showed his displeasure with N58.4 billion debt servicing saying,

> *"I am not comfortable about this, 'why is it that the masses have to suffer because of debts incurred by government's careless expenditures?"*[3]

This situation no doubt, has increased the inflation rate in Nigeria. According to the former Central Bank of Nigeria

113

2. John Stott, Issues facing Christians, Marshall Pickering, 1984, p. 212
3. African Concord, Vol. 7, No. 39, February 15, 1993

Governor, Abdulkadir Ahmed, between 1986 to 1992, annual rate of inflation grew from 5.4 percent to 46 percent. "This in a large measure" he pointed out, contributed to the depreciation of the value of the naira. He also pointed out that at the end of 1992, the nation's domestic debt stood at N160.10 billion, with N136 billion or 85 percent owed the Central Bank of Nigeria by the government – this is the result of what he called, "high-powered" money obtained through "ways-and-means" advances.   This   the   CBN   governor admitted, had advanced effects on inflation, balance of payments and the naira exchange rate[4].

The above are just examples of the situation in Nigeria where individuals are richer than the nation itself and is also quite clear from the above why it is so. It has been emphasized from time to time that one individual or few Nigerians will be capable of paying the Nigerian debts without pains. The major example was how politicians spent money in last unsuccessful electoral process.

It is true that we cannot say that it is only in Nigeria that this problem of poverty and inflation is high. However, still one would not really agree with one Brother Leo Barrington, in his report in which he writes: concerning foreigners and wealth, he says:

> *"Another illusion that quite a number of*
> *people suffer under is to think that all*
> *foreigners are wealthy and possess plenty*

114

4.   Newswatch, March 8, 1993, CF also John Darnton's report in the New York Times, January 5, 1977, that every 1,000 Nigerian babies die before the age of five, and half of that before the age of five, and half of that before the age of one. 40 percent death rate to 3 per cent U.S. No. 1606, Sun. December 26, 1993, 1984, p. 143.

of money. Many times I have been asked for enormous sums of money. A thousand pounds sterling – 700 US dollars. Quite impossible figures. But there is one thing very pleasing about Nigeria, which really puts it apart from so many others. You do not find many beggars. If I go to Cairo, or to Algeria, or Napoles or Paris I will often be besieged by suppliants. From time to time, I go to Paris, last week when traveling on the Netro in Parish I was five times accosted by beggars who said they were starving[5] "

The above assumption could not be far from that of the self-exiled Umaru Dikko who in 1983 stated concerning the dwindling economy of Nigeria then that no Nigerian was picking from the dust-bins, but eating off the bins. But still there are those living in over affluence.

The kind of society we live in is made for affluence and this has resulted to other vices. William Barclay quoted K. Rice as saying:

"The things which are flouring amidst our prosperity are veneral disease, mental disorder, bad debts, juvenile delinquency, drug addiction, strikes, bankruptcy, crime "[6]

5. "Independent" Catholic Weekly News, No. 1606, Sun. December 26, 1993, P. 9
6. William Barclay, <u>Ethics in a Permissive Society,</u> Fount paperback, London, 1984, P. 143

In Nigeria, the crime rate has reached epidemic level. Drug trafficking has become institutionalized that today a Nigerian on international trip becomes an object of ridicule through search. Not only in drugs, Nigerians are now international and local fraud stars; a household word in Nigeria today is "419" which even crepped into the Christian Church. Newswatch of March 8, 1993 carried a report titled "Nigerians with ugly Faces", "The bad Nigerians" the report states, are having a hell of a time in Austria doing bad businesses: prostitution, drug trafficking and "419". It also states that daily, more Nigerians are being arrested, jailed or deported by the Australia authorities for all shades of economic crimes. Hardly a week passes without a newspaper reporting a case of a Nigerian caught for a crime or the other[7]. The paper also reported that in most European countries, prostitution is big business, and that a powerful international syndicate made up of link men and women now exists whose work it is to lure young girls from Nigeria with false job promises, arrange all travel documents and trade them with operators of brothels and producers of blue films and nude photographs. Newswatch, it stated, learnt that in Australia, a link man or women is paid N14, 000 for every three girls.

The paper also noted that in their attempt to seek greener pastures overseas, some Nigerians have become very desperate. They have tried various ingenious methods, sometimes unsuccessful to beat immigration officials of their

116

7. Newswatch, op.cit, p. 20

host countries. After giving examples of individuals involved, the paper says; "Such is the extent Nigerians have gone to either get out of the country or survive in foreign land". In "most of the countries", the paper went on, "Nigerians have been subjected to all kinds of ill-treatment because of the atrocities of a few. In Austria, for example, Nigerians are no more granted refugee status. Newswatch reported that in the last six months (for the time of this report), more than 100 Nigerians seeking to be admitted into the refugee camps have been deported. About 900 Nigerians are currently in that country's refugee camps. The paper further reported that Lateef Jakande, former Lagos State Governor, traced the problem to its roots, and said, "The government has to improve living conditions within the country. This will dissuade economic migrant from not only exposing themselves to unnecessary hardship abroad, but also prevent them from soiling the country's image in the desperation to improve their economic well-being. If we cannot do this, then we should not complain about the harassment of our citizens[8].

The economic hardship in Nigeria coupled with the hoarding of wealth by some have led a lot of Nigerians to be "checking out" like "Andrew". There are in-security in every segment of our society. Lack of job, the educational system has crumbled, no proper road net-work, no good electricity supply, no proper road network, no good electricity supply, no pipe-bone water. The dwelling places of so many people cannot be

117

8. Ibid, p. 21

easily called houses in the true sense of it. For instance, in Lagos which for so many years was capital of Nigeria you may find about as many as ten adults and children living in a room. In this same Lagos where so many people live under bridges, you still see so many magnificent mansions and luxurious apartments like the ones in Ikoyi, Allen Avenue, Ikeja, Victoria Island, etc. In most of these, the latest in-household luxuries are installed including in some cases sauna baths, some with stand-by generators to give light. There are families who have living-in-maid, good food to eat and transports to move with. To most of them holidaying abroad for summer and taking treatment abroad, even delivering babies abroad is never a problem. That is the same Nigeria. You wonder how they make it. It has reached to the stage that it appears before one can survive in Nigeria you have to be –put plainly-corrupt.

Engineer J.A. Jege in expressing his feelings about corruption in Nigeria in an articles "Surer way out of corruption in Nigeria" states as follows. That there is no way you can want many cars, many houses, many wives, many children without being corrupt (going by the average legitimate Nigerian income). That corruption is a by-product of underdevelopment and the African culture (though one may not totally agree with him especially on culture). That Nigerian Christian prays to God to give him money, houses, cars, wives et al, while the English Christian prays to God to enable him live such a good life of love and service to humanity here, so that later in heaven he can reign with Christ. He also stated that the structure in Nigeria has created way for corruption. He gave example of the director general who after extorting his own share from the contractor hands him over to the director, the secretary, the clerk and the messenger for them all to extort theirs in turn before the contractor gets his cheque and another case of a director general who insists on the proper procedure for awarding contracts being strictly adhered to while his governor has awarded or is planning to award nothing about construction works. The governor becomes furious and sacks the director-general or re-assigns him[9].

The situation is serious in Nigeria that we now have what is called "the Nigerian factor", so that if Nigeria decide to fight corruption, who will bell the cat? Chief Ernest Shonekan in his maiden address to the nation when he took over from Babangida as the Interim Head of State said, that anyone who wishes to fight corruption in this nation must have the moral right to do so. The question is who has the moral right? In Nigeria if one is asked to catch a thief, he steals the stolen good. An example of this is reported in the Tempo Magazine of 13, January, 1994, titled, "The Billion Naira Fraud – twenty –four hours. After the NDLEA seized N44 billion worth of drugs, a fraction of it remains unaccounted for – a report by Seye Kehinde[10]. This same issue of the often his appearance of drugs seized by the Agency as in recent times

119

9.   J.A. Jege, "Sure way out of Corruption in Nigeria", in the Nigerian Christian, vol. 26, August 8, 1993, pp. 3-5
10. Tempo magazine, 3 January 1994.

says the report, led to a source of irritation between the Agency and its foreign advisers which has indeed led to the suspension of further support from them.

The Churches in Nigeria are not exonerated from these lifestyles that pervade our society. The Nigerian Evangel of July-August 1993, reported of a United Baptist Church Pastor along Mission Road Benin-City who defrauded the Church N0.5 million[11]. So many others use different tricks to defraud people in the name of praying for them or seeing visions for them. We discuss more of this in chapter four of this book. The struggle to make it by all means in Nigeria has given rise to so many finance houses. Most of them promising even above 50 percent interest. For an example, a well-known Umannah E. Umannah of Resources Managers Limited who was arrested and detained from October 28 to November 1991 in Port Harcourt in whom was found about 50 million and above according to report in TSM by Comfort Obi[12].

It can be said with truth that the struggle for the acquisition of wealth is mainly the causes of our present political predicament in Nigeria. People are interested in sharing the national cake without thinking of its baking. This was the type of struggle that led to the civil war in Nigeria. In this section of the world, it is practically taken for granted that the highest possible ambition for anybody is to become a millionaire. This is so because in Nigeria one is measured by how materially wealthy you are. Chieftaincy in the society and

11. The Nigerian Evangel, Magazine of the Church of Nigeria (Anglican Communion), July-August, 1993, Vol 1, No. 2,p.9
12. Report by Comfort Obi: TSM –The Sunday Magazine, vol.4, No 19, November 17, 1991

in the church is given to the highest bidder. The political power in this country is based on how rich you are (the money bags) and not how wise or faithful you are; how international connected you are and not how locally concerned you are. If you are able to loot the treasure of the government, you can come around dash them N50 – N50 to the poverty-ridden Nigerians, and they would proclaim you their messiah not counting your past. To be appointed to any service in Nigeria today means to every Nigerian, "Let him go there and take his share" hence embezzlement everywhere. The recent revelations through the panels of inquiries set up by the government of Nigeria into the parastatals shows that all (without exception) the heads of the parastatals have embezzled the public fund left in their care, starting from NNPC, NIPOST, NITEL, NEPA, NPA, CBN, NAN, etc. The common site in Nigeria today is burning of public houses starting from finance and audit department in order to cover up fraud.

Nigeria also suffers under the market economy. The situation has rendered the economy useless and worse. This has been blamed on the capitalist scene. Dr. Jonathan Silas Zwingina examined the influx of capitalist economy in Africa, in particular Nigeria, and how this was being legitimized in Nigeria by the indigenous bourgeoisie in collaboration with their foreign allies and concluded the process as problematic[13]. But some economists have blamed the situation of Nigeria on

13. J.S. Zwingina, Capitalist Development in African Economy, University press, PLC, Ibadan, 1992, p. 254.

reckless spending of various government agencies, scandals of various kinds as mentioned earlier. It is this spirit of capitalism that could be responsible for materialism in the life of Christians in Nigeria.

Although many of the capitalist economic tenets, and indeed the philosophical ones also, have some things in common with Christianity, the basic point of disagreement is over the value place on the individual. Though there are much flaws in capitalism, socialism like communism has not been found to be appealing or even successful instead it has been found to be a total failure like in Russia and China. Thus, many Christians have been turning away from communism and capitalism searching for alternative with the hope that something new may be discovered. Some suggest Welfarism.

Indeed, the instinct of self-preservation and realization remains an ineradicable part of human nature. Nevertheless, the more mature a Christian is, the more he might, opt for a solution that could enhance a better relationship. One essential requirement of a system for a Christian is that the personal advantage never involves the sacrifice of any other, or (if it is) a question of one's business thriving at the expense of another's, because the later is not strong or not managerially efficient or lack dynamic leadership. There ought to be some ways of safeguarding those who suffer[14].

According to John Stott, the inequalities within the nation are neither political nor economic, but moral problems.

122

14. Derek Farrow, Through the eye of a Needle, Epworth press, London, 1979, P. 98

Until we feel moral indignation over world-wide social injustice, and compassion for world-wide human suffering, we are not likely to act[15]. Derek Farrow states that there is need to change any economic system which brings harsh condition upon many[16]. An alternative must be discovered.

Due to the harsh economic situation in Nigeria, people have resorted to so many unchristian system of wealth creation, such as gambling[17], cheating, hoarding and the like. It is a pity on the way people hoard or lavish money in Nigeria while a lot suffer in abject poverty. Materialism, that is, the use today, Affluence could never satisfy restless hearts. Affluence helps to deprive one billion hungry people of the world of badly needed food and resources. Will the affluent Christians have the courage and faithfulness to learn how to be un-conformed to this world's seductive satanic advertising[18]?

Wealth is the chief idol of the present Nigerian. Its glamour has led us into very many troubles. Christians have great role to play in order to bring about a harmonious society and establish a Nigeria where justice and equity shall reign. Poverty is not the will of God for man and therefore, we must pray and seek for the will of God to be done on earth.

5.2   THE SITUATION OF THE POOR

In today's world especially Nigeria, poverty has reached such proportions of high rate of suffering, child malnutrition and mortality and it is exerting, such a destructive potential

15.   John Stott, op.cit.,p. 136
16.   Derek Farrow, op.cit, p. 104
17.   Oji Onoko, "More than Chance", African Concord vol. 7, No.39, February 15, 1993.
18.   Roland J. Sider, The Rich Christian in an age of Hunger, Paulist press, New York 1977, p. 50

that it has indeed become children's greatest enemy[19]. Poverty is hitting hard upon over two-thirds of the world's populations and so affecting every sector of mankind, families and communities as a whole. It has reached an epidemic state in Nigeria.

Hunger and malnutrition are noticed all over the world especially in under-developed countries. A 1974 UNICEF study reported that about 224 million of Indian's 600 million people consumed less than 75 percent of the caloris they needed. A WHO study claims that about 30 percent of sub-Saharan African's children do not get the needed nutrients. The result is pre-mature death for some, and for many others, life-long hunger, mental and physical retardation[20]. The chronically hungry have less resistance to disease and are more susceptible to parasites. Hunger is a bad disease in itself, "a hungry man" they say is an angry man.

This was what Jesus noticed on the faces of the crowd that followed him and he was moved by compassion to make sure they were fed. Food is really important to human living hence Jesus thought in the Lord's Prayer: "Give us this day our daily bread". (Luke 11:3). One greatest danger of the world's happiness today is famine[21]. The growth in population especially in Nigeria is getting more than the growth in food production and this compounds the problem more. To feed the millions of mouths, the country is forced to produce more and to consume less. The result is that there are more desperately

19. IYC and WCC report on the World Council of churches, International tear of the child, p. 3
20. Charles Elliott, "Patterns of Poverty in the third- the earth is the Lord's (ed.) Mary Evelyn, Jegen and Bruno V. Manno, Paulist press, NY. 1978, P. 150.
21. Kevin M. Gachill, Famine, Orbis Book, Mary Knoll, N.Y. 1982, P. 63.
       22.

poor people in Nigeria today than there were twenty years ago.

This is scandalous. The Bible does not romanticize poverty. In the Old Testament it is seen as a curse to be poor (2 Samuel 3:29, Psalm 109:9-11). Sometimes poverty is seen as a result of sin. A fundamental point in the book of Job is that poverty and suffering are not always due to sin. They can in fact, be redemptive as in the suffering servant of Isaiah 53. Even so, poverty and suffering are not inherently good and desirable. They are tragic distortions of God's good creation[22].

Poverty is caused by ultra-individualism. That is due to the selfishness of man or the fall of man, so poverty is not of God and is very degrading to man.

There is no such a thing as virtue of poverty. Jesus never idealized poverty; rather he came to liberate the poor. His gospel is to uproot all injustice and exploitation and bring friendship and love. The Bible speaks of liberation and justice as opposed to the slavery and humiliation of the poor in history. The gift of Sonship is accomplished in history by accepting others as our brothers and sisters we accept this free gift not in word but indeed.

In Nigeria, it is an incontestable fact that the bulk of the population are suffering from social structures and particularly acts of oppression that forces on them a denial of justice and a fragmentation of their solidarity. These are also

125

22. Ronald J. Sider, op.cit. P. 127

people who we recognize the love of God for them. They need the church to come to their aid.

Let it be noted here that it is a heresy to think that wealth are always a sure sign of righteousness and blessing. In fact, they may even be the result of sin and oppression. The crucial test is whether the wealthy are obeying God's command to bring justice to the oppressed. God wills prosperity with justice, and God wills justice for the poor.

5.3   OPTIONS FOR RICH CHRISTIANS

In current situation of pursuit for affluence and living in affluence, there are three options open to Christians. The first is to become voluntarily poor, the second is to stay rich, and the third is to cultivate generosity, simplicity and contentment.

First, Voluntary Poverty: Paul wrote, "For you know the grace of our Lord Jesus Christ, that though he was rich, yet for your sake he became poor, so that you through his poverty might become rich" (11 Corinthians 8:9). Also in Philippians 2:5-8), he stated, "have this one mind among yourselves, which is yours in Christ Jesus, who though he was in the form of God, did not count equality with God a thing to be grasped, but emptied himself, taking the form of a servant being born in the likeness of man. And being found in human form he humbled himself and become obedient unto death, even on a cross".

This voluntary self-impoverishment of Jesus was the theological ground on which the apostle based his appeal to the Christians of Greece to contribute to the relief of the Christians of Judea[23]. It is also upon this that he would wish Christians to live as if they possess nothing, having the mind of Christ. To have the mind of Christ means: that the character of Jesus Christ should be the standard of the Church, and there is this unique feature which Paul calls 'Mind' – which the community of God's people is to experience. It is this very aspect of Christ's character which is most threatened in godless contemporary society[24]. It is this type of mind that Christians ought to apply in our present day Nigeria.

It is this theological conviction that led some early Church fathers to take up voluntary poverty. The earliest Christian book of Christian teaching, the Didache says, "Do not parade your own merits, or allow yourself to believe presumptuously, and not make a point of associating with persons of eminence, but choose the companionship of honest and humble folk[25]. The poor then were seen as the basis of a new community in Christ. To attack the poor is to attack the Lord of the Church, not only harming mutual relationships but, according to James 2:7, committing sacrilege as well. Still at a stage in the Church, the poor became neglected. The gap between the rich and the poor came also into the Church.

As a result of this, some Christians decided to share in the fate of the poor, taking the way of voluntary poverty. Like

23. John Stott, op.cit., p. 223.
24. Howard Snyder, New Wineskins: Marshall Pickering, London, 1987, P. 113.
25. The Didache", Early Christian Writings, Frans, Maxwell Standiforth, Penguin, pp. 228-229.

St Paul of Thebes in the middle of third century, they made their home in the desert, thereby keeping alive the ideal of poverty as a reminder of the original clarity and radicalism of the gospel[26].

Still most of the poor people did not choose poverty freely. It was a lot imposed on them by the powerful who did not wish to share their power and wealth. Sometimes these poor organized movements of resistance against social injustice. The Church position had been somewhat between voluntary poverty and these movements opposed to poverty. The church attempted sometimes through noble acts, to Christianize and thus humanize society and its institutions among other things. This was after the recognition of Christianity as official religion of the Empire in Rome. The Church then distributed wealth more fairly through organized charities. Notable among people who began this move were Ambrose, the fourth-century Bishop of Milan, Basil, the archbishop of Caesarea who established the first hospices and refugee shelters[27].

From the sixth century, to the eight century, the poor man was the traditional model of the half-starved creature, the beggar, the victim of the exactions of the officials and the calamities of civil wars: this is the picture painted by Gregory of Tours in his history of the Franks. There were also the impoverished serfs of province and the artisans of Arles, whose archbishop St Caesarius preached to in direct and practical

26. Coemaad Boerma, The Poor Side of Europe, WCC Publication Geneva, 1989, P. 17.
27. Ibid P. 18

style; he gave the poor help of a different kind by freeing prisoners from the Goths. Pope Gregory the great, in Rome, assisted victims of plague and famine[28].

This age gave rise to monastic life. We have people like St. Francis of Assisi who abandoned all his possessions because of the poor in Assisi. He was supposed to have had this dialogue with Christ: "You are mad, Francis". "No more than you are, my Lord". Without a touch of such madness, the current of poverty which reached its point in the thirteenth century not have become such a mighty river whirling along and overflowing its banks. The life of St. Francis touched many in his generation up-till now.

So many others went this way for example, Robert d' Arbrissel and Etienne de Muret, the Canons of Premontre, Arnold de Francisca and Henn de Lausanne St. Alexis, Peter Waldo the Hermit, Valdes and Francesco Bernardone[29].

The value of poverty (that is voluntary poverty) was that it is Christ way of life and this made it a worthy choice for anyone. Also the fact that Christ had been subject to it made living in poverty a trial for salvation, and helping the poor a redemptive work. A keen awareness of the sufferings of the poor meant that benevolence was based both upon justice and upon charity[30].

"Poverty of Spirit" has an important place in spirituality but is not a sufficient basis for the church in the socio-economic order. The possession of wealth by proxy, or

28. Michael Mollat, "Poverty and the Service of the Poor in the History of the Church", The Earth is the Lords, (ed), mary Evelyn Jegena nd Brun V. Manno, paulist Press, N.Y. P 48.
29. Ibid, P. 51.
30. Ibid, P. 52.

physical or moral person, is no longer an adequate way of justifying the status quo. Organizations representing the Church still hold enormous wealth both in Nigeria and outside. Public opinion is rightly less concerned about the amount of wealth accumulated by a religious organization and the economic power this gives it, than about the way they use the money. Does the Church simply use it to enrich itself, or to serve the common good and in particular to help the poor? Ecclesiastical pronouncements and speeches are often evasive on this point[31].

It could be necessary to point out here that possession has taken the heart of man instead of God and except this is repudiated, then we have no portion with God. A.W. Toser says: "Our woes began when God was forced out of His central shrine (the heart) and things were allowed to enter. Within the human heart things have taken over[32]. Therefore, Christians could begin to learn to surrender and sacrifice for the sake of the underprivileged.

The example of Jesus, the teaching and practice of the early Church challenge Christians to renounce covetousness, materialism and luxury, and to care sacrificially for the poor. But these do not establish the case that all Christians must be materially poor.

Second option for rich Christians in Nigeria is the opposite of the first – to remain or stay rich. Like had been stated earlier in this book most of these Christians defend

---

31. Hubert Le pargneur, "The Problem of Poverty and How the Church can help, The Earth is the Lord's op.cit., P. 92.
32. A.W. Tozer, The Pursuit of God, Scripture Union Press and Book Limited, Ibadan 1987, p. 21.

themselves by appealing to the portion of the bible which tend to say all material possessions are blessings from God. The recent evangelists in Nigeria preach it and live it. It is a common thing these days to preach in the screen of the television where they would be seen. After each programme, they invite people to send letters with their seed-money so that the programme may continue. The Church has always been somewhat schizophrenic in its approach to material wealth. The middle ages gave us both gilded basilicas and ascetic monks. The Church today especially in Nigeria looks more and more like the world. It may be true that if the Church tends to the way of the world, the world is more likely to listen to it. As Sernau puts it, "The greatest hurdle we face in presenting the gospel in the western world (like in Nigeria) is not ignorance, but cynicism, the great unmet need is not so much for people to hear the gospel but to see the gospel, 'To see it in us'. Cut crystal is a poor substitute for shining stars"[33].

This was the kind of problem Timothy faced amidst the wealth and poverty of the urban world of first century Ephesus, Paul's reminder to him can be a reminder to us all, and if we clinch to wealth we shall lose it.

Now we come to the third option which is to cultivate generosity, simplicity and contentment.

Let us look at Generosity: This is a special duty laid down upon every Christian right from the Old Testament period. It is part of a good man's duty to maintain the rights of

131

33. Scott Sernau, <u>Please Don't Squeeze the Christian into the World's Mold,</u> Inter Varsity press, Illinois, 1987, P. 57.

the poor and needy (Proverbs 31:9). He does not close his eyes to the crying of the poor (Psalm 82:3, 4). The case for the poor was laid down in the Old Testament not only as a duty to man, but also as a duty to God.

A Christian ought to find it very difficult to develop a concept of absolute ownership. He recognizes that God himself is the true owner and he is merely a steward. Therefore, he holds anything as a responsibility. The more wealth or power a person achieves, the more his personality develops on attitude which assumes power and more as of right without question. Here begins the well-known process of corruption which is attributable to power. Wealth breaks through the Gordian Knot of ever-increasing complication and allows a Christian, if he has wealth or power, to sit lightly upon it, to accept it while it is his, to accept its removal if that is to be, he is released from the intensity of trying to keep what he can, and thus from the absolute corruption that ultimately awaits him[34].

The Christian wealthy must see it as a burden on him to share. Christians must develop an understanding of stewardship that relates humans to the resources that sustain that life. It is a critical task that must be done. To neglect the impoverished of the world is to defy God (cf. Matthew 25 and 1 John 3:3). George S. Siudy Jr. says:

> *"Responsible behaviour is responsive behaviour toward God, the neighbour, the earth, and oneself"* – and *"Stewardship is*

34. Derek Farrow, op.cit. p. 121

action that anticipates answers to our questions, fully senses social solidarity and accords with the dependence of human life upon the earth and upon God".[35]

Frantz Fanon makes the point clear.

"The question which is looming on the horizon is the need for a redistribution of wealth. Humanity must reply to this question or be shaken to pieces by it.[36]

Human beings are called to be agents of the divine plan and, in co-creative partnership, to share God's continuing creativity. God not only limits and orders our life, but creates conditions of its opportunity. "Behold I have set before you an open door, which no one is able to shut" (Revelation 3:8). Christians have so many open doors to be generous to one another. Stewardship views the possession of wealth not as selfdom, nor merely as trusteeship, but especially as opportunity[37] so it urges generosity.

As Christians – people who are bought with a price- the attitude to giving must be to present everything to Christ. It is not just ten percent, but hundred per cent should be God's portion and this is the beginning of Christian stewardship. There should be no legal restrictions to the generosity of a Christian, for, "where the Spirit of the Lord is, there is liberty" (2 Corinthians 3:17). Paul who, himself was a Jew and a Pharisee never once mentioned tithing yet still he dealt with

35. George S. Suidy Jr. "Stewardship and World Poverty", The Earth is the Lord's, op.cit p. 152.
36. Ibid. P. 153.
37. Ibid P. 154

money within the context of the freedom men had to give or not give as the Holy Spirit led[38].

"Malachi and its tithing text is found in the Old Testament which calls man to prosperity" says G. Lewis, "Put the New Testament, with Christ as its example, calls men to adversity. Paul says that "all that will live godly in Christ Jesus shall suffer persecution" (2 Timothy 3:12). A man who is prosperous never feels persecuted. Adversity in God's blessing for the New Covenant. To appeal to man to give in order that he might be prospered is in profound effect to deny a man the true riches and blessings which are found in Jesus Christ[39]. A Christian in his generosity would not mind laying everything down when the need arises.

There must be the letting go (Mathew 6:19-21), Luke 10:29f, 12:29-32). We need a re-awaking of Christian values which emphasizes the responsibility of each for the care of the common goods for the good of all. There need to be created a world system which can best translate the saving and sharing of Christians into available resources for the use of others[40].

St Paul summons Christians to be both generous and contended. In 1 Timothy 6:17 and 18, he asked Timothy to "command those who are rich...to be rich in good deeds, which is to be generous and willing to share. For by that they are like God who gives generously. Then he went further to make it clear that contentment is necessary for every Christian. He says in 1Timothy 6:6-10 "There is great gain in godliness

38.   Honest Uche Nwosu, Long Essay: "The Christian Concept of giving and Stewardship, with Particular reference to Anglican Diocese of Owerri, Department of Religious Studies, University of Ibadan, 1991, pp. 168f.

39.   Gregory Lewis, Is God for Sale? Is God for sale Tyndale House Publishers, Inc. Whealon, Illinois 1979, P. 105.

40.   S.O. Abogunrin "The Community of Goods in the Early Church and the Distribution of National Wealth", Religion and National Unity (ed) Sam babs Mala orita, Ibadan, 1988, P. 93

with content, for we brought nothing into the world, and we cannot take anything out of the world; but if we have food and clothing with these we shall be content. But those who desire to be rich fall into temptation, into snare, into many senseless and hurtful desire that plunge men into ruin and destruction. For the love of money is the root of all evils. It is through this crawing that some have wandered away from the faith and pierced their hearts with many pangs.

It is covetousness to scramble to amass wealth. It seduces the heart from love for God and imprisons it in love for money. Then this call here for contentment and simplicity of life is ideal and is the secret of inward peace[41]. Human life is a pilgrimage from one moment of nakedness to another.

Bishop John V. taylor felt that the word poverty has become negative and extreme in its sound in our present ears hence he prefers the word "simplicity", because it puts emphasis on the right points..."Our enemy", he said, "is not possessions, but excess. Our battle cry is not "nothing" but "enough"[42].

Simplicity in a private dimension has to do with our ability to let go to detach ourselves from material possessions, and even from the desire for them. Simplicity in a social dimension is a life lived low for the sake of other[43]. Whatever a man's treasure is, if it comes before God in his heart, then he must "give it away". If Christians in Nigeria today are to follow that commandment – love your neighbour as

135

41. John Stott, op.cit P. 228
42. John V. Taylor, Enough is Enough, SCM Limited, London, 1975, pp. 81, 82
43. Adam Daniel Finnerty, No More Plastic Jesus, Orbis Books, Mary Knoll, New York, 1977, P. 105.

yourselves- if we are really "to love our neighbour as ourselves", Christians will recognize that the world is urgently in need of simple life-style on the part of the people of God.

Let us quickly discuss some of the dangers inherent in wealth.

5.4   INHERENT DANGERS OF WEALTH

Jesus himself did not appear to regard the acquisition of wealth as evil in itself. He appears even to regard wealth and the acquisition of wealth as something which could be used to win friendship in this life and commendation in the life hereafter (Luke 16:9).

While Jesus exhorts men to exert themselves to produce wealth, which will enable them to live in an abundant world, equally and frequently he warns them of the dangers that are in it. Some of the dangers of wealth are:

(1)   Obsession:

We can be so much obsessed by material possession that we discover that it commands our allegiance and cripples our faith[44]. Wealth has its subtle way of becoming one's master. For where your treasure is, there will your mind also be. Whatsoever that takes first place in our heart is Lord at that time. Concerning divided loyalties, D. Bonhoeffer wrote: "Earthly goods are given to be used, not to be collected. In the wilderness God gave Israel the manna every day, and they had no need to worry about food and drink. Indeed, if they kept

136

44. Scott Sernau, op.cit. P. 59

any of the manna over until next day, it went bad. In the same way, the disciple must receive his portion from God every day. If he stores it up as a permanent possession, he spoils not only the gift, but himself as well, for he sets heart on his accumulated wealth, and makes it a barrier between himself and God. Where our treasure is, there is our trust, our security, our consolation and our God. Hoarding is idolatry[45].

(2)   Wealth could cripple faith in God:

There is the tendency for an abundance of possessions to lead one to forget that God is the source of all good. One may trust in self and wealth rather than the Almighty God. (Deuteronomy 8:11-17). In his statement on this, Richard Foster says: "If what we have we receive as a gift, and if what we have is to be cared for by God, and if what we have is available to others, then we still possess freedom from anxiety. This is the inward reality of simplicity. However, if what we have we believe we have gotten, and if what we have is not available to others, then we will live in anxiety. Such persons will never know simplicity regardless of the outward contortions they may put themselves through in order to live "the simple life"[46]. Most of the rich people are too busy to give their services to God.

(3)   The pursuit for wealth often result to war and neglect of the poor: (James 1-2).

Riches often harden the hearts of the wealthy toward the poor instead of fostering more compassion. (See examples

137

45.   Dietrich Bonhoeffer, The Cost of Discipleship Macmilliam, New York, 1963, P. 194.
46.   Richard Foster, Celebration of Discipline, Hasper and Row, San Francisco, 1978, P. 77

in Luke 16:19-31, Isaiah 5:8-10, Amos 6:4-7 and James 5:1-5).

R.J. Sider quoted Don Holder Camara, a Brazilian Archbiship who has devoted his life to seeking justice for the poor, as making the point forcefully: "I used to think, when I was a child that Christ might have been exaggerating when he warned about the dangers of wealth. Today I know better. I know how very hard it is to be rich and still keep the milk of human kindness. Money has a dangerous way of putting scales on one's eyes, a dangerous way of freezing people's hands, eyes, lips and hearts[47].

Many in high social positions are sick of vanity. They are longing for a peace which they have not. Many of the greatest scholars and statesmen, the world's most eminent men, will in these last days turn from the light, because the world by wisdom knows not God[48].

The New Testament sees riches as capable of begetting arrogance in their possessor and subservient snobbery to those who come into contact with him. The New Testament is well aware of the attitude of mind which riches can produce both in the mind of the man who has them and in the minds of the people they come in contact with[49].

Riches are something which man cannot trust because they are not permanent or stable. A man's life cannot be assessed by it. It is a diminishing asset. The desire for wealth can blind a man to the higher things and a man will die without the riches with him.

47. Ronald J. Sider, op.cit, P. 122
48. Ellen G. White, Christian Service: General Conference of SDA Washington, D.C. 1949, P. 204.
49. William Barclay, op.cit P. 155

Further to the dangers of wealth, William Barclay outlined as: (a) something that beget a false sense of independence, (b) that there are times when money can cost too much, like the case of Judas Iscariot. (c) The more a man possesses in this world, the more difficult it will be for him to leave it. (d) One of the curious results of wealth is that it is very liable to produce in a man, not the comfortable feeling that he has enough, but the constant desire for more[50].

Having known how dangerous materialism is, it behooves on all Christians in Nigeria, not necessarily to become poor, but to cultivate generosity and simplicity with contentment, shunning avarice and greed. We need to concentrate on the necessities of life and not luxuries. For it is hard to be wealthy in Nigeria without getting soiled.

5.5   POVERTY AND THE CHURCH IN NIGERIA

The role of the Church in relation to the Nigerian society in general can differ both in principle and in historically demonstrable concrete models. The present complementary relationship belongs in this context. The church is queried about its acclaimed uniqueness, its understanding of man in relation to the world founded on belief in Christ, and about the emerging implications for the dignity of man and his right.

The Church is certainly capable of making an essential, contribution to the issue of fundamental human values. The

139

50.   Ibid., P. 168

Christian understanding of God, life, and man, is universal and central. Therefore, the contribution of the Church to value orientation affects man, nature and the environment, it also affects the present, past and future, the individual, and society as a whole over all groups and differences.

In terms of the content of its witness of faith, the Church ought to make important contribution to the enhancement of the total well-being of mankind. Christian faith is not only concerned with a defined religious province, but rather, with all of reality, because God in Jesus Christ granted salvation to the whole world. The summary of the Christian law is "love the Lord your God with all your heart, soul and mind – then love your neighbour as yourself. It is a vertical and horizontal relationship. The possibility of a positive decision in the conflict situation of borderline ethical problems is formed by the Christian faith.

The Church's witness concerns the basis and limitation of freedom just as much as it does the basis and limitation of authority. According to faith and the gospel of the Church, justice is constructively creative, it is not only judging, but also saving, not only reacting. God's justice opposes all arbitrary partiality, regardless of the reasons. According to the gospel of the Church, solidarity is not only an ultimately exclusive social responsibility of the inner group based on sympathy, social responsibility, but also is comprehensive, transcending race, class, nation and supranational blocs[51].

51. Hans Thime Bielefeld, "The Churches of Jesus Christ and the condition of man in society" Universitas A Quarterly German Review of the Arts and Science Special Edition, pp. 233-237.

We in Nigeria are experiencing a time of <u>kairos</u>, that is, a very propitious moment for proclaiming the gospel, for furthering the Church's life. Attention is needed in this situation with the spread of the good news for the poor. The option for the poor must involve recognition of the need to have a change in structures or systems of oppressions. The option for the poor and the oppressed through a liberating commitment cannot be isolated from the social set up to which they belong otherwise we would not go beyond, "being sorry for the situation". The poor man therefore is someone who questions the ruling social order. Solidarity with the poor implies the transformation of the existing social order[52].

The newness of the recent contrasts of wealth and poverty call for the Church's conscious response. The Churches have the gracious duty, as part of their prophetic ministry, of denouncing the iniquity of concentration of goods in the hands of the few, the injustice in unequal distribution of resources which the humblest have helped with their sweat and their blood to create closer to the different realities of each situation, the local Churches are better placed to speak out more accurately and specifically. They can only accomplish such mission to the extent that free from compromise with the political and economic powers they be, they can collaborate in freeing those whose lot they share. Only the free can set free[53].

But can the Churches have the moral right to fight or struggle for the poor when they marginalize them? The

141

52.   Anthony J. Tambasco, "Option for the Poor", The <u>Deeper Meaning of Economic Leif,</u> (ed) R. Bruce Douglas U.S. Catholic Bishops' Pastoral letter on the Economy, P. 47.

53.   Fernando Bastos de Avila, "Church and World Hunger", <u>The Poor and The Church</u> (ed) Nobest Greinacher and Alois Muller, A Cross Road Book, the Seabury Press, New York, 1979, P. 6.

Church, Kumba Cameroon conference, affirmed possesses everything in Christ, but she should fight indefatigably so that there is an equitable distribution of her material resources, before she can ask the state to do the same. This is one of the central affirmations formulated by some 300 pastors' full-time treasurers, Church dignitaries and social workers of the Presbyterian Church in Cameroon[54].

Gustavo Gutierrez says that many Christians have recently been becoming more and more aware that if the Church wants to be faithful to the God of Jesus Christ, it has to rethink itself from below, from the position of the poor of this world, the exploited classes, the despised races, the marginal cultures. It must descend into the world's hells and commune with poverty, injustice, the struggles and hopes of the dispossessed because of them is the Kingdom of Heaven. It basically means the Church living as a Church the way many of its own members live as human beings; being born again as a Church means dying to a history of oppression and complicity. It is not a question of the Church being poor, but of the poor being the people of God, the disturbing witness to the God who sets free[55].

The gospel tells us that the signs of the arrival of the Kingdom is that the poor have the gospel preached to them. Perhaps we should go further to say that the preaching of the gospel will be truly liberating when the poor themselves are the preachers. In contrast to our flamboyant preachers today

142

---

54. Report: "Church Richer than it Thinks", by A Cameroon Conference, Economical press service, Geneva 28, February. 1980, No. 6 47th year, P. 5.
55. Gustavo Gutierrez, "The Poor in the Church", in the Poor and the Church.

who care less about the poor. Whoever sees them as being poor says it is as a result of their sins or their laziness. However, when the poor preach this gospel would it be acceptable to the "Affluent society of ours"? It would sound local, but that is how the Lord would speak to us. Only by listening to this voice will we recognize him as Saviour. This voice speaks "In ecclesia" with a different tone. Therefore, if the Church gives a place to the poor then it is really a Church.

One would say here that the first missionaries to Nigeria had a sense of mission to the poor. According to A.C. Krass, they tended to become multi-purpose missionaries. They preached the gospel which they had been commissioned to do, but they also transcribed languages, developed literary materials, started schools, set up hospitals to cure the sick, took part in agricultural development, settled disputes, and often judged court cases. Many of them began local industries. The Church was doing and paying for much of the work for which governments are responsible today[56].

We can say that the mission-oriented denominations in Nigeria had made a lot of contribution in the past to the liberation of the poor especially by the provision of social amenities. Bishop Olajide of Ibadan Church of Nigeria (Anglican Communion) stated that the Church had been making its impact felt in the provision of social enhancement for the poor. He said for instance, that the Anglican Church started the school of the deaf and the dumb in Ibadan. That

143

56. A.C. Krass, Go and make Disciples, SPCK, London, 1974, P. 155

another center for the handicap has recently been established by the Church at St Luke's College, Molete, Ibadan. He still maintained that the Anglican Church in Nigeria has an inbuilt system in each parish in aid of the poor to which each pastor is responsible and he wished the Church could do more especially in her healing ministry[57].

The other Churches like the Roman Catholic Church, the Baptist Churches, the Methodist Church, etc. have different centers where the less privileged are taken care of and the Scripture Union Nigeria has ministry that reaches out to the poor, <u>according to the former General Secretary, Brother Chris Okeke</u>[58].

Let us consider here that the Church is still very much lacking in its response to the yearning of the poor. The power of poverty as a sign has decreased in our modern society, both among the rich and among the poor. Poverty has no prophetic forces except in sermons – if it is preached at all. Even in the Roman Catholic Church, none of the three vows of religion is respected and valued in the same way as it was even thirty years ago.

If the Church proclaims liberation, it must give an example of freedom and independence from economic and political worldly powers. This means it rejects certain easily available but dubious financial assistance. In the last chapter of this book we shall make a little appraisal and suggestions to the problem of Wealth and Poverty.

57. G.O. Olajide (Rt. Rev'd). Interviewed 28th January 1994 (the Anglican Bishop of Ibadan).
58. Brother Chris Okeke, Scripture General Secretary, interviewed 28th January, 1994.

6

THE WAY FORWARD

All that this topic has been about is to make the Nigerian Christians understand what was Jesus' attitude to wealth and poverty and to know how Christians especially in Nigeria ought to apply themselves to it.

We inched toward this truth. To believe in God is to live our lives as a gift, and to regard all that happens as a manifestation of that gift. Slowly we came to understand our arrogance hubris according to the Greeks. When we go beyond the human measure, reality has a way of bringing us to our heel. When we believe ourselves to be titans and act accordingly, we are shortly reduced to our true helplessness. It is exactly in that helplessness that one lives the first beatitude[1].

1.   Philip Berrigan and Elizabeth Mc Alister The Time's Discipline: The Beatitudes and Nuclear Resistance: Fort Kamp Publishing Co. Maryland 1989. P. 27

We discovered in this book that poverty is merely a distribution problem, and therefore of domination and we could discover that unemployment which is an agent of poverty is a structural problem. This is so because, it is caused not only by human plans and choices but, above all, by economic and political systems which entail a larger or smaller proportion of the labour force remaining outside the labour market. This is also an ethical problem for its causes and effects, as well as its remedies have to do with human plans and choices and it deprives people of one of the most fundamental ways of fulfilling themselves. It is also a theological problem because it involves God's will for his kingdom. It is so because it is a subject with which the word and action of the building of the kingdom of God as revealed in Jesus, is concerned[2].

We discovered how dangerous possession could be to a Christian and then Christians in Nigeria are challenged to a right attitude to wealth. They are to avoid materialism as it is being peddled today even in the Church. Christians are to rise up against the unjust distribution of wealth. Christians should take seriously the possibility that the present serious recession is due to God's judgment on our greed; because we have not honoured God in our economic life, he has given us over to the consequences of our passion to possess.

We must note that in history, we learn how dangerous prosperity is. It is not the men who have lost their money and

2. Ignacio Ellacuria "Unemployment" Unemployment and the Right to work Ed. Jacfues Pohier & Dietmar Mieth T & T Clark Edinburgh 1982 P. 91.

their prosperity who are in the greatest danger, but those who have obtained a fortune and are placed in higher position. These need careful and earnest labour. Adversity may depress, but prosperity elevates to presumption. Therefore as we talk of the care for the poor, we must remember the rich to whom Jesus said, "Woe to you who are rich...(Luke 6:24). The men who are exalted and praised need greater help. There are thousands of rich men who are starving of spiritual feed. Few among them go to Church; for they feel that they receive no benefit[3].

The Christians must follow the example of Jesus Christ in all his humility and concern for the poor. If Christianity is characterized by its universal claims, whether made on the basis of creation or of the final consummation, what affects majorities should be a principle governing the degree of authenticity of historical verification of this universalism. These majorities are not only sum total of individuals who are poor and outcasts as individuals, but also collectives made up of social groups[4]. The Church needs to be socially involved in the total liberation of mankind.

Poverty does not bear witness any longer to anything especially among the poor and it does not witness to the rich either. However, this new ethos does not entirely discount the value of evangelical poverty which is often the price of bearing witness because anyone who covets power, advancement, money, prestige or position does not have the inner freedom

3. Ellen G. White Evangelism: Review and Herald publishing Association Washinton, D.C. 1970, Pp 155, 561.
4. Jeh Sobrino The Dignity of the Despised of the Earth: The Seabury press New York P. 13 See 1 an H. Boer, Missions Day Star 1984 pp. 158-165.

needed for justice and the Gospel. Or else evangelical or voluntary poverty is the necessary condition of being listened to in certain contexts. The world expects the Church and its clergy to speak, more truly, live more authentically, work more effectively to help the oppressed and the weak, rather than just be poor themselves. In Nigeria the poor are often deprived of their goods to decorate Churches and endow the clergy. They have never demanded that their clergy should be poor but that they should be upright and devoted.

The Gospel must not be measured with any form of worldly standard, for its effectiveness does not coincide exactly with worldly efficiency. There is a lot of obsession with visible efficiency (worldly) leading to a large scale investments – enterprising – this risks the loss of any real efficacy of the gospel. Still the gospel needs material and human resources to operate – but there must be a balance. The Church activity should not be in competition with the secular or with one another; it should be directed towards service. The work being done and the witness such work bears to the gospel should be tested from time to time by public opinion. Worldly standard of fund generation must be avoided.

The Church needs to set up a programme for the poor. Here Prof. S.O. Abogunrin suggests, that we need to evolve a new economic system that would bridge the gap between the rich and the poor majority. He does not support the religious obligation of giving alms to beggars by the road side and in religious houses; the building of 'rehabilitation centers which in the long run becomes like prison yards as solution to poverty problem in Nigeria. He urged a close examination of some Nigerian colonizing others in their land.

The call is not that Christians should be poor or the clergy, to be poorer than the poorest, but their individual and collective lifestyle should show a general austerity, in accordance with their personal or communal vocations. The clergy on their own must bear witness by their thrift, careful administration without being either mean or merciless, generous sharing, according to their particular sphere of action in the Church and the world. The right use of the wealth of a religious community should act as an example of what should be expected in civil society. Religious communities also normally bear witness by the good they have done throughout their history.

The poor we always have with us. Hence the care is the responsibility of every Christian. The poor in Nigeria are yearning for those who will speak on their behalf. Poverty is a social and spiritual question and the Church must not shun its responsibility. The Church is in a privileged position to make meaningful contribution. It is in fact present on both sides of the trench, in both camps of the conflict between poverty and wealth. It is with those who go without, the starving, and the oppressed, whose needs and demands it can make explicit. The Church can be and has been the voice of those who have no voice of their own. However it is also with the affluent and the oppressors, whose consciousness it can trouble with the voice of the oppressed and it cannot abdicate from this mission without abdicating from its prophetic mission.

It should, like John the Baptist, call the people to order. It should like Jesus ask for more work of mercy than law. Poverty problem must concern the Church and Christians in general. Faced as it is now, with the gravity of the scandal of hunger, the Church today in Nigeria is being challenged to advance beyond the realm of pronouncement into that of prophetic action; such action may be one of voluntary shedding of worldly good which would also have symbolic value and place the Church firmly in a position of commitment to those who suffer injustice. If it could not be easy to wipe out hunger within the structure and dynamic of an unjust and predatory social system, then it is an ethical imperative for our age to look for, and find an alternative system[5].

We have to conclude this write up by joining in this kind of prayer. "Yet I envy the rich man too some of the time. Riches are relative to regions, and this is a wealthy region. What is an abundance in one area is average here. I look at the storehouse, newly built, and have wished they were mine.

What good a man could do!

How much freedom he would have!

What possibilities would be opened!

If only, if only the wealth here is mine!

150

5.   Fermando Bastos de Avila "The Poor and the Church", "Church and world Hunger", Ed. Norbert Grevnacher & Alois Muller Cries Road Book N.Y. 1977 P. 78.

Yet deep down I know that, given a sufficiently life of any quality is something that is beyond riches. Deep down I know that whatever goods I possess only whet the appetite for more. The other man's grass is always greener. Life cannot be packed into barns, hoarded against perpetual rainy days. The life you give a man is the real wealth, Lord. It is the wealth of meaning, of hope, of joy, the wealth of faith, of affirmation, of love, the wealth of life eternal for which a man might even be prepared to die. Bring me near to this man, Lord, near to yourself.[6]"

6. Rex Chapman A Kind of Praying SCM London 1970 P. 26

AFTERWORD

By
Venerable Professor Samuel Ike
Enugu. December 2014.

Have you been longing for a compendium in which the Old Testament concepts of wealth and poverty are married together with Jesus application of these, in a manner practically relevant to today's realities? Yet all this in a flowing easily readable style; the book, Jesus Attitude to wealth and poverty, has provided that.

In Jesus Attitude to Wealth and Poverty, Ven. Dr. Honest Nwosu has put down a compilation that is at once a theological treatise as well as a practical guide to a basic need and practice in the church and society. Here is an x-ray into the many sided presentations of what remains topical in our spiritual and mundane pursuits.

We have here a detailed enquiry into the various shades and meanings of words that represent and typify wealth and poverty in the Old Testament of the Bible. We also read Jesus teachings and implied attitude to both of these, as well as other relevant New Testament references to them.

This book is also replete with a survey of distortion of the prevailing teachings on matters of prosperity and poverty, while situating these with the apt balance required. It also interrogates author's views and cultures as extensively as it does the economic principles and forces at play today controlling issues of money and acquisition.

This book is a must-read for the householder trying to make ends meet, and for the student of economics; for the Christian and minister of the gospel seeking balance and Jesus attitude on issues of wealth and poverty. The business owner and the corporate players will find a veritable working tool here, just so as the ardent researcher on concepts of wealth and poverty will discover here a rich exegesis of much informed literature.

May the profound, balanced and insightful truth presented by this compilation be a helpful guide to the enquirer, and serve to prepare your heart, attitude and life for "the treasure where no moth can devour and no rust affects" in eternity, in Jesus name. Amen.

BIBLIOGRAPHY

A. Books

Angel C.R.,   **The Price Tags of Life:** Broadman Press. Nashville.

Ashton Cyril,   **Servant Spirit – Serving church:** Marshall Pickering U.K. 1988

Barclay William: **Ethics in a permissive Society** Fount Paperbacks, Glassgow, 1971.

Barclay William   **The Plain Man's Guide to Ethics** Fount paperbacks, Glassgow, 1973.

Barclay William: **The Plain Man Looks at the Lord's Prayer:** Fount paperbacks, Glassgow, 1964.

155

Barclay William: **New Testament words SCM,** London, 1964.

Barclay, William: **The Gospel of Matthew** Vol. 1 Westminster press, Philadephia, 1975.

Barclay William: **The Gospel of Luke:** The Westminster press, Philadephia, 1975.

Barrel, E.V. & K.G. **ST Luke's Gospel:** John Murray, London, 1992.

Baster, nancy: **Distribution of Income and Economic Growth Concepts and Issues** Geneva 1970.

Beiden A.D. et al   **The Rebel Church :** James Clarks, London

Blanch Stuart: **Way of Blessedness:** Hodder and Stoughton, London, 1985.

Blanch Staurt: **Encounters with Jesus:** Hodder and Stoughton, London, 1088.

Bonhoeffer Dietrich: **The cost of Discipleship.** SCM press,

London, 1959.

Bockle Franze ed. **War, Poverty, Freedom** vol. 15 Paulist Press. New York.

Boarma Coenraad: **The Poor side of Europe** WCC, Geneva, 1089.

Boice Mantgomery J: **The Sermon on the Mount** Ministry Resources Liberary, Grand Rapids, 1988.

Brgant Darrol: **To whom it may concern: Poverty Humanity and Community** Roetress press, Philadelphia, 1969.

Bruce Birch C. et al.: **The Predicament of the Prosperous.** Westminister, 1978.

Bruce Nichollass ed. **In words and deeds. Evangelism and social responsibility:** The Patnernoster press, Australlia, 1985.

Cahill K.M. ed **Famine:** Orbis Books Maryknoll, New York, 1982.

Cassidy Michael: **The passing summer:** Hodder and

Stoughton, London, 1989.

Chardwick Owen: **Western Asceticism:** SCM, London, 1958

Chapman Rex: **A kind of Praying** SCM London 1970.

Cho Yongi Paul: **Salvation, Healh and Prosperity**. Crusader Books, Umuahia, Nigeria 1987.

Clark Henry: **The Christian case against poverty** Asscoiation press. New York 1965.

Door Donal: **Option for the poor: A hundred years of Vatican social teachning** Gill a Macmillian, Dublin, 1983.

Douglas Bruce R. Ed. **The Deeper meaning of Economic Life:** Cath. Bishop letter on Economic.

Douglas W. Johnson: **Managing change in the church**: Freindship press New York 1974.

Farrow Derek: Through the eye of a needle Epworth press, London, 1979.

Finaerty D.A.   **No more plastic Jesus** Orbis Books

Maryknoll, New York, 1977.

Pletcher W.M.   **The Second Greatest CommandmentL** Navpress USA, 1983.

Foster Richard: **Celebration of Discipline**: Harper and Row, Sanfranscco 1978.

Foulkes Francis: **How the goodness began: Study Guide to Mark's Gospel**. African C. Press Ghana, 1985.

France R.T.   **Jesus the Radical :** Inter-varsity press, London, 1989.

Freeman H.E.   **Every Wind of Doctrine:** Faith Builders Publication, Aba; Nig. 1987.

Fuller H.R. & Brain K.R. **Christianity and the Affluent Society**, Holder and Stoughton, London, 1966.

Galbraith J.K.   **Affluent Society:** Penguin, London, 1962.

Gatites Segundo: **The Beatitudes:** Orbis Books Maryknoll,

New York, 1984.

Gooding Daving: **The Gospel According to Luke**: Intervarsity Press, London, 1987.

Gordon Andrew S.T. **Security Freedom and Happiness** Catholic Social Guild, Oxford, 1944.

Grassi J.A.   **Broken Bread and Broken Bodies the Lord's Supper and World Hunger** Orbis Books, Maryknoll, New York, 1985.

Green Michael: **Evangelism New and Then**: Inter-varsity press, London, 1979.

Green Michael: **Matthew for today:** Hodder and Stoughton London, 1988.

Greet G.K.   **When the Spirit Moves** Epworth press, London, 1975.

Greinacher Norbert & Muller A. Ed. **The poor and the Church** A cross Road, Book. The Seabury Press. New York 1977.

Griffiths Michael: **Down to earth God:** Hodder and

Stoughton, London, 1986.

Hall P.C. | **Human values and Advancing Technology:** Freindship press, New York, 1967.

Heilbroner R.L. | **The making of Economic Society:** Prenticehall, New Jersy, 1968.

Henry Carl. F.H. | **Christian Personal Ethics** Baker Book House, Michigan, 1957.

Hengel Martin: | **Property and Riches in the Early Church, Aspects of A Social History of the Early** Church: SCM Press, London, 1974.

Holman Robert: | **Poverty: Explanations of social Deprivation:** Martin Robertson London, 1978.

Houston Tom: | **Characters Around the Cross MARC:** Eastbourne 1986.

Hunter A.M.: | **Interpreting the Parables:** SCM Press, London, 1964

Hunter Leslie: **The Seed and the Fruit**: SCM Press London 1957.

Jegen Evelyn Mary & Bruno V. Mammo, Ed **The Earth is the Lords** Paulist Press New York 1978...

Johnson L.T. **Sharing Possessions: Mandate and Symbol of Faith:** Fortress Press Philadelphia 1981.

Keller P.W. **Layman Looks at the Lord's Prayer:** Moody Press, Chicago, 1976.

Kempis Thomas A. **The Immitation of Christ:** Fount paperback 1963.

Knox J. **The Ethnics of Jesus in the teachning of the church** Epworth, London 1962.

Kirk A. **A new world coming:** Marshalls London, 1983.

Krass A.C. **Go-and make Disciples:** SPCK London. 1974.

Lewis G. **Is God for sale?** Tyndale, Illinois, 1979.

Lindsell Harold: **The World, the Flesh and the Devil:** Canon press, USA 1973.

Lockyer H.   **All the Parables of the Bible** Zondervan. Michigan, 1963.

Mala Sams ed.   **Religion and National Unity:**   Orita, Ibadan 1988.

Macquarrie J.   **Three Issues in Ethics: SCM Press** London 1970.

Malherbe J.A.   **Social Aspect of Early Christianity** Fortress press, Philadelphia, 1983.

Manson T.W.   **The Teaching of Jesus:** Cambridge University Press, London, 1963.

Mcminn G.& Libby L.   **Choosing to be Close** Multnomah press, Portland, 1984.

Metcalfe J.   **The Beatitudes:** The publishing Trust Buckinghamshire London, 1993.

Miller D.G.   **Saint Luke:** SCM press, London 1960.

Moule CFD: The birth of the New Testament A & C, Black, London, 1981.

Needham D.C.   **Birthright:** Multnomah press, Portland, 1979.

Newton A.J.   **The Fruit of the Spirit in the lives of Great Christians:** Epworth press, London, 1979.

Neibuhr R.H.   **The Social Sources of Denominationalism.** Henry Holt. New York 1957.

Nolan Albert: **Jesus before Christianity:** orbis Books, maryknoll, new York, 1976.

Nwosu, H.U.   **Honesty as the Way of Life:** Emuje press: Akure 1 1988.

Ojo, A.F.   **Gripped by Greed:** Gospel Publication International, Ibadan, 1992.

Olukolade Shola: **Your Power to get wealth** Pentecostal Publishers, Lagos, 1992.

Osthathios Mar Gee Varchese: **Theology of a Classless** orbis Books, maryknoll New York, 1979.

Pemberton P.L. & Finn R.D.   **Toward A Christian Economic Ethics** Winston press, N.P. 1985.

Polie J & Mieth D.   **The Dignity of the Despised of the Earth**. The seabury press, new York, 1979.

Polie J and Mieth D. **Unemployment and the right to work.** T & T. Clark, Edimburgh 1982.

Ramsey Michael: **Sacred and Secular:** Harper and Row. New York.

Ravenhill Leonard: **Why Revival tarries:** Send the light trust, London, 1972.

Redpath Alan: **Blessings out of Bufferings**:   Pickering and inglis, London, 1981.

Sanders O.J.   The Best that I can be Scripture Union (nig). Press Ibadan 1985.

Sanner A.E.   **The Gospel of Mark:**   Beacon Hill Press. Missouri, 1979.

Santa F.G.   **Modern Study in the Book of proverbs**: Mott Media USA 1978.

Sernau Scoth: **Please don't squeeze the Christian into the world's mold:**   inter-varsity press, unions, 1987.

Sider J.R.   **Rich Christians in age of Hunger** Paulist press, new York, 1977.

Sider J.R.   **Christ and Violence:**   Herald press Canada, 1979.

Siyder Howard: **New-wineskins:**   Marshal pichering London, 1984.

Sheen J.F.   **Life of Christ**: BN Books, London, 1958.

Shepherd David: **Bias to the Poor:** Hodder and Stoughton London 1983.

Stanforth Maxwell Fr. **Early Christian Writings:** Pengium Book, London 1981.

Stewart J.S.   **The life and teaching of Jesus Christ.** St Andrews press, Edimburgh 1965.

Stiver L.R. Hunger,   **Technology and Limits to growth:** Augsburg publishing House, Minneapolis, 1984.

Stett John   **Issues facing Christians today:** Marshall Pickering, London, 1984.

Swindoll, C.R.   **Growing Strong in the season of Life:** Multnomah, Portland 1983.

Taylor V.J.   **Enough is Enough** SCM, London, 1976.

Tidball Derek: **Messengers of Goodnews:** Scripture Union, London, 1991.

Tozer A.W.   **The Pursuit of God:** Scripture Union (Nig) press, Ibadan, 1987.

Vaughan B.N.Y.   **The Expectation of the Poor** SCM. 1972.

Walker Andrew ed.   **Different Gospels:** Hodder and Stoughton, London.

Weber Max: **The Protestant Ethics and the Spirit of Capitalism:** G. Allen, London, 1930.

Wenham David: **The Parables of Jesus:** Hodder and Stoughton, London 1989.

Wilcock Michael: **the message of Luke,** Inter-varsity press, London, 1979.

Wilton Robert: **Dare to be a Success:** Beulah land publishers, Benin, 1987.

White E.G. **Evangelism:** Herald publishing Association, Washington D.C. 1946.

White E.G. **Education:** Pacific press, Ontorio, 1952.

Wright Christ **Knowing Jesus through the Old Testament:** Marshal Pickering London, 1992.

Ziesler J.A. **Christian Asceticism:** SPCK London, 1973.

Zwingina J.S **Capitalist Development in an African Economy.** University Press, Ibadan, 1992.

B.　DICTIONARIES AND COMMENTARIES

Longman Dictionary of Contemporary English Ed. Paul procter: Longman, England, 1978.

The American Heritage Dictionary of the English Language: Ed. William Morris, Houghton Mifflin, New Jersey, 1981

Cassells English Dictionary: Ed. Atthur L. Hayward and John J. Sparkes, Cassels, Longon, 1979.

The Compast edition of the Oxford English Dictionary: Vol II: Oxford University Press, London, 1971.

The New World Dictionary Concordance to the New American Bible: World publishing Times Mirror, New York, 1970.

The Interpreter's Dictionary of the Bible Vol. 3 ed. George Arthur Butbric et al. Abingdon press, New York 1962.

The Interpreter's Dictionary of the Bible Vol. 4 Ed. George Arthur Buttric et al. Abingdon Press, New York, 1962.

The Interpreter's Dictionary of the Bible: Supplementary Vol. Ed. Keith Crim et al. Abingdon, New York. 1976.

New Bible Dictionary 2nd edition: J.D. Douglas et al. Intervarsity press, London, 1982.

Dictionary of Christ and the Gospels Vol. II Ed. James Hasting: T & T. Clark Edimburgh, 1962.

The International Standard Bible Encyclopedia Vol. II Ed Geoffrey W. Bromiley: The Paternoster Press, Exter 1982.

Encyclopedia of Religion and Ethics Vol. 12 ed. James Hastings: T & T Clark, Edimburgh, 1958.

The Lion Encyclopedia of the Bible, Special Edition; Ed. Pat Alexander et al. Lion Publishing, England, 1986.

Encyclopedia of Biblical Theology Ed. J.B. Bauer. Sheed & Ward; London, 1970.

New Bible Commentary 3rd Edition: Ed. D. Guthrie et al. Intervarsity Press, England, 1982.

Mathew Henry's Commentary on the Whole Bible: Ed. Leslie F. Church; Marshall Morgan & Scott, London, 1960. the Jerome Biblical Commentary Vol. II ed, Raymond Brown et al. Geoffrey Chapman, London, 1980.

C.   JOURNALS AND DAILIES AND PERIODICALS

Universities: A Quarterly German Review of the Arts and Science, Special Edition.

Theology Digest: Vol. 35, no. 1. Spring 1988.

Theology Digest: Vol. 22, No. 4; Winter 1974.

Theology Digest: Vol. 22, No 2; Summer, 1974

Official Gazatte: Vol. 65. No 14, 29th March, 1978.

Vintage Peoples: Vintage Ventures publications Vol. 1 No. 34, march, 30 – April 5, 1990.

Christian Treasury: An Independent Christian Magazine Dec. 1993. African Concord Vol. 7. No 39, Feb. 15, 1993.

Newswatch, Nigeria's weekly Newsmagazine: Newswatch Communications, lagos, March, 8, 1993.

Newswatch: February 7, 1994.

New York Times: Jan, 5, 1977. New York

Independent: Catholcis Weekly News No. 1606, Sun. Dec. 26, 1993.

The Nigerian Christian Vol. 26, Day Star press. Ibadan, August 8, 1993.

Tempo Magazine: 13. Jan, 1994.

The Nigerian Evangel: Vol. 1, No. 2. Magazine of the Church of Nigeria (Anglican Communion) July – August 1993.

The SUndary Magazine Vol. 4. No. 19, TSM Publishers: Nov. 17, 1991.

IYC. And WCC Report on world council of churches International Year of the child.

D.   **ARTICLES, REPORTS AND INTERVIEWS**

Alexander A.B.D.   **"Wealth" in Encyclopedia of Religion and Ethics Vol. 12:** James hasting; T & T Clark, Edinburgh, 1958.

Abogunrin S.O.   "The community of Goods in the Early Church and Distribution of National Wealth" **Religion**

and National Unity Ed. Sam. Mala Orita, Ibadan, 1988.

Bastes de Avila Fernando "The church and world hunger" **The poor and the church** Ed. Norbert g & Alois. M. Seabury Press New York 1979.

Bielfeld H.T. "The Churches of Jesus Christ" and the Condition of man in society" Universities: A quarterly, German Review of the Arts and science special edition.

Congar Yves: "Poverty in Christian life amidst an affluent society" War, Poverty, Freedom Vol. 15 ed. Franse Bostle paulist Press, New York, 1966.

Ellacuria Ignacio "Unemployment" **Unemployment and the Right to work** ed Jacques Pohier & Dietmar Mieth; T & T. Clark, Edimburgh, 1992.

Elliott Charles: "Patterns of Poverty in the third world" The earth is the Lords ed. Mary. E.J. & Bruno V.M. Paulist press, new York, 1978.

Gutierrez Gustavo "Liberation Theology" **Thoelogy Digest** Vol. 35, No. 1 Spring, 1988.

Hellman Wane: "Poverty: The Franciscan way to God" <u>Theology Digest</u>. Vol. 22. No. 4 Winter, 1974.

Jeje J.A.   "Sure way out of corruption in **Nigerian Christian** Vol. 26 Daystay press, Ibadan, August 8 1993.

Lee   Gary   A.   "Goods"   **International   Standard   Bible Encyclopedia Vol. II** Ed. Geoffrey W. Bromiley et al.   Willian Eerdmans publishing England 1982.

Le. Pargneuer Hubert "The problem of Poverty and how the church can help" **The earth is the Lord's** Ed. Mary Evelyn Jegen & Bruno V. Manno Paulist press. New York. 1978.

Mallat Michael   **"Poverty and the service of the Poor** In the history of the church" The earth is the Lord's Ed. Mary and Bruno. Paulist press New York 1978.

Onoko Oji   "More Thannchance" African Concord Vol. 7, No. 39, Feb. 15, 1993.

Obi Chioma   "Riddle of the Celestial Church harvest Candle."

Vintage People Vol. 1 No. 34. Vintage Ventures Publications, Lagos. March 30 April 5, 1990.

Okeke Chris General Secretary Scripture Union (Nigeria) Interview, 28 Feb. 1994.

Olajide G.O. The Bishop of Ibadan; church of Nigeria (Anglican Communion) Interviewed 28 Feb. 1994.

Robert Koch "Riches" **Encyclopedia of Biblical Theology** Vol. 11 ed J.B bauer sheed and Eards London 1970.

Siudy G.S. "Stewardship and World Poverty" **The Earth is the Lord's**; Ed Mary Evelyn Jegan and Bruno V. Manno, Paulist press. New York. 1978.

Tembasco A.T. "Option for the Poor" The **Deeper meaning of Economic Life** Ed. Bruce Doyglad. U.S. Catholic Bishop's Pastoral letters, 1989.

Torrance J.A. "The Theology of Liberation in latin American" **Different Gospels**. Ed Andrew Walker Hodder and Stoughton London 1988.

A Cameroon Conference: "Church Richer than it thinks" ecumenical **Press Service:** No 6. 47th year, Geneva, 28 Feb. 1980.

E.   UNPUBLISHED WORKS

Ekennia U.A.   Christianity and Wealth **A Sociological Approach M.A.** Dissertation to the Dept. of Religions Studies. University of Ibadan. Nov. 1990.

Nwosu H.U.   **The Christian Concept of Giving and Stewardship with Particular Reference to the Anglican Diocese of Owerri.** B.A. Long Essay submitted to the Dept. of Religious Studies, University of Ibadan. 1991.

www.ingramcontent.com/pod-product-compliance
Lightning Source LLC
La Vergne TN
LVHW011232080426
835509LV00005B/463